# FORENSICS:
# SOLVING THE CRIME

## Acknowledgments

My profound thanks to Benjamin T. Lonske, Ariana A. Yeatts-Lonske, Catherine F. Wingfield-Yeatts, Helen D. and Harry W. Yeatts Sr., Latanya R. Walker, Amile R. Somers, Amanda Lloyd, Mara Patzig, John Paul Osborn, Sir Alec Jeffreys, Patricia Albright and Sue Towle of Mount Holyoke College Archives, Ron "Bonedoc" Armstrong, Dr. Fred Armitage of King's College London, Kevin Leonard of Northwestern University Library Archives, Stuart S. Kind, Albert Simpson, Dr. Midori Albert, Michelle V. Buchanan, Atlanta Sisters in Crime, New Scotland Yard, and especially Harry W. Yeatts Jr.         — *Tabatha Yeatts*

## Dedication

This one is just for Dashiell.

*Paul A. Osborn (center), grandson of forensic pioneer Albert S. Osborn, introduces his grandchildren, Christopher and Elizabeth, to the forensic science of examining documents.*

# FORENSICS:
# SOLVING
## THE
# CRIME

## Tabatha Yeatts

*The Oliver Press, Inc.*
*Minneapolis*

The Oliver Press, Inc.
Charlotte Square
5707 West 36th Street
Minneapolis, MN 55416-2510

————————

*Excerpt from THE CENTURY OF THE DETECTIVE by Jurgen
Thorwald, © 1964 by Droemersche Verlagsanstalt A. G. Zurich, English
translation by Richard and Clara Winston © 1965 by Jurgen Thorwald,
reprinted by permission of Harcourt, Inc.*

————————

*Library of Congress Cataloging-in-Publication Data*
Yeatts, Tabatha.
Forensics : solving the crime / Tabatha Yeatts
p. cm. — (Innovators ; 8)
Includes bibliographical references and index.
    Summary: Profiles eight pioneers in forensics, including James
Marsh (toxicology), Henry Faulds (fingerprints), Albert Sherman
Osborn (questioned documents), Charles Waite and Calvin Goddard
(ballistics), Mildred Trotter (forensic anthropology), Jacques Penry
(Photo-FIT), and Alec Jeffreys (DNA fingerprints).
ISBN 1-881508-75-7 (library binding)
1. Forensic scientists—Biography—Juvenile literature. 2. Forensic
sciences—History—Juvenile literature. 3. Criminal investigation—
History—Juvenile literature. [1. Forensic scientists—Biography. 2.
Forensic sciences—History. 3. Criminal investigations.] I. Title. II.
Series.
HV8073.8 . Y43 2001
363.25—dc21
                              00-052858
                                 CIP
                                 AC

ISBN 1-881508-75-7
Printed in the United States of America
07 06 05 04 03 02 01          8 7 6 5 4 3 2 1

# CONTENTS

# Using Science to Investigate Crimes

When a crime has been committed, law enforcement team members have many methods to discover who is responsible. First, they gather information by interviewing potential witnesses and others who might know either the victims or the suspects. Investigators may also search records to see whether similar crimes have been committed in the area and whether a pattern exists among the crimes.

Secondly, police officers gather physical evidence at the scene of the crime. They often erect barriers around the area to keep evidence from being removed, changed, or lost. The police also want to ensure that no false evidence is introduced into the crime scene—for example, an item that would make an innocent person appear to be guilty. They usually photograph the scene before carefully removing and labeling evidence.

Once the physical evidence has been properly assembled, experts are brought in to analyze it.

*Hands gloved, these forensics experts carefully search a crime scene.*

**evidence:** anything that could help decide the guilt or innocence of a person suspected of a crime

Forensics can also refer to the art of debate.

Some evidence is obviously important, such as a bullet or a blood stain or a fingerprint. A clue can also be a plain and ordinary object—a piece of paper or some carpet threads. Finding what information a clue can reveal is a key part of forensics. The work may seem dull and painstaking . . . but this field of science can also perform magic.

The term "forensic" comes from the Latin *for ensis*, meaning "public forum," and actually refers to anything to do with courts of law. In police work, forensics is science that has been applied to questions of civil and criminal law.

When a forensic specialist uncovers details about a piece of evidence, the police can use this information to understand what took place at a crime scene. Forensic specialists provide law enforcement organizations with a vast array of information about casework under investigation. They can compare traces of hair, grease, paint, or glass left at a crime scene with those found in a suspect's possession. They can offer information about what an explosive was made of, how a fire started, what kind of tire left a track in the dirt, and where soil on a shoe came from.

Forensic scientists must be just as at home in a courtroom as in a laboratory because they may be called upon to give their conclusions in court—for either the prosecution or the defense. When scientific evidence is presented in court, experts must have reached their opinions by methods that have proven reliable and that were properly conducted using working equipment run by a qualified operator. They must present their conclusions without regard to the desires of the prosecution or the defense but with dedication and trust in their work.

Forensics has traveled a long road to become the well-established, exciting field that it is today. Throughout the ages, people have wanted to investigate suspicious deaths, as well as find ways to look into other types of crime. Lack of scientific knowledge, however, prevented many forensic specialties from advancing until the nineteenth or twentieth century.

The first known autopsy—an examination of a dead body to determine the cause of death—took place in 44 B.C. in ancient Rome. After dictator Julius Caesar was stabbed to death in the senate house by a number of his friends and senators, a physician named Antistius determined that only one of the 23 stab wounds caused his death. For hundreds of years after Caesar's murder, however, autopsies remained unpopular in many cultures because of the widespread belief in the importance of keeping the dead intact.

**autopsy:** post-mortem (after death) examination of a body, usually by a doctor who specializes in this branch of science, known as a medical examiner

The position of coroner, an appointed official who holds inquiries into unexpected deaths, is one of the oldest public offices, dating back to about A.D. 900 in England. The first coroners were "keepers of the pleas of the crown," later shortened to "crowner," then "coroner."

The book credited as the first written forensics work appeared in 1248 in China. Entitled *Hsi Duan Yu (The Washing Away of Wrongs)*, the book described ways of discerning natural deaths from unnatural ones. For instance, it suggested that damaged cartilage on the neck and pressure marks on the throat indicated death by strangulation.

A significant technological development for forensics occurred in 1590 when Holland's Zacharias Janssen created the first compound microscope, which used two or more lenses. It was a much more powerful tool than the single-lens microscope already in use. People heard about this new invention quickly, and interested scientists, such as the astronomer Galileo Galilei, strove to make their own. But it wasn't until the second half of the seventeenth century that the microscope became an important scientific tool to study microorganisms or blood.

*This compound microscope was used by medical students in the 1870s.*

In 1810, when the first detective organization began in France, the police had few forensics tools available. But simply creating a special crew to handle the investigation of crimes was an important step in law enforcement. This first organization came about in an unusual way. Escaped convict Eugène François Vidocq had approached the police with an offer of help because he wanted to remain free of the threat of returning to prison, as well as have the chance to settle scores with his underworld enemies. The police agreed, hoping to use Vidocq's in-depth knowledge of French criminals. Vidocq proved sincere in his desire to be on the right side of the law and eventually supervised a force of 20 detectives later known as *la Sûreté*, or Security. Like Vidocq, all were former criminals.

Vidocq had a thousand ruses. He regularly planted his men into prisons by sham arrests, and extricated them again by sham escapes or even simulated deaths. In this way he obtained an unending stream of information.
—Jurgen Thorwald, author of *The Century of the Detective*

Photography was just beginning to develop at this time, and it was not yet a forensics tool. So Vidocq would make trips to the prison to look at

*Originally jailed for beating a man, Eugène François Vidocq (1775-1857) broke out of prison twice. His methods were bold and clever, but he was caught and returned to prison with additional time added to his sentence. Vidocq escaped a third time in 1799 and remained a hunted man until 1810, when he offered his services to the police.*

the inmates carefully in order to commit their individual features to memory. He was famous for his memory. He also created an archive of drawings and descriptions of known criminals and their methods.

Across the Atlantic Ocean, another famous detective agency began in 1850 when Scottish immigrant Allan Pinkerton founded Pinkerton's National Detective Agency in Chicago, Illinois. The agency collected information about thousands of known criminals for its national crime file. New advances had made photography useful in forensics, not only for identification of criminals, but also for crime-scene

Kate Warne, Pinkerton's first female detective, was hired in 1856. Pinkerton considered her one of his best operatives and had her head his "Female Detective Bureau." He was ahead of his time—police departments did not allow women to join their ranks until 1891.

documentation. By 1870, Pinkerton's had what was said to be the country's largest collection of mug shots—photographs of people charged with crimes. Police departments from all over the United States requested information from the agency's file.

Back in France, a young records clerk struggled to update the identification system begun by Vidocq. In 1879, Alphonse Bertillon (1853-1914) developed an anthropometric system of criminal identification.

*The Pinkerton agency's office logo inspired the term "private eye" for private detective.*

ESTABLISHED IN 1850

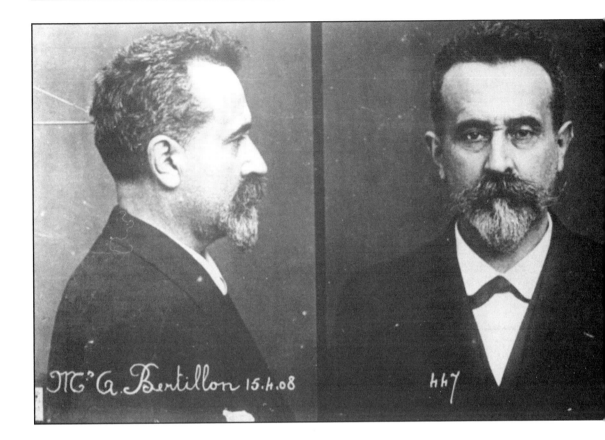

After arresting a suspect, police took a series of body and facial measurements—for example, circumference of the head, length of the feet, and length of the ears. Called "Bertillonage," this system was widely used until fingerprints became an accepted forensics tool in the early 1900s.

In 1910, also in France, Edmond Locard (1877-1966) established the world's first forensic laboratory. Locard proclaimed the "principle of interchange," still cited today, which states that a person committing a crime always leaves something

*Alphonse Bertillon also introduced the practice of full-face and profile photographs of suspects to aid identification. This is his own police portrait.*

**anthropometry:** the study of human body measurement used by anthropologists to compare and classify human beings

*Edmond Locard believed that a criminal always leaves a piece of evidence at the scene.*

behind at the scene and always carries something away. The search for that small something—trace evidence such as dirt, hair, or cloth fibers—is a large part of contemporary police work. And when such evidence is found and analyzed, it can often lead police to the culprit.

Another milestone in the field of forensics was reached in 1923 when the *Frye v. United States* case set the standard by which courts admitted forensic evidence. The ruling by the District of Columbia Circuit Court acknowledged that it is difficult to know when a scientific discovery goes from being "experimental" to "demonstrable." The principle the court settled on was that the discovery "must be sufficiently established to have gained general acceptance in the particular field in which it belongs." Using that criterion, the court ruled in *Frye* that polygraph (lie detector) tests were not admissible evidence. Many states today still do not allow polygraph results to be submitted in trials.

In 1975, the Federal Rules of Evidence (FRE) were introduced. These rules apply to federal cases only, although some states also use them. Rule 702 states that if scientific or other specialized knowledge will help the court to understand the evidence or answer a question, "a witness qualified as an expert by knowledge, skill, experience, training, or education, may testify . . . in the form of an opinion or otherwise." This overrode *Frye's* "general acceptance" rule and adopted a "relevancy and expertise" standard.

There are many different forensic fields, and they have progressed at different speeds. Yet technological and scientific advances that help one area often help another. The development of the microscope, for example, was very important to both firearm and questioned document examination. Photography became integral to fingerprinting as well as facial identification. Advances in chemistry were essential to toxicology (the study of poisons) and to DNA testing.

The work of forensic pioneers could not have been achieved alone—they needed the contributions of other scientists to build on and the aid of law enforcement and the legal system to bring their work to fruition. Many people played a part in making modern forensics vigorous and indispensable.

The path that forensic trailblazers traveled was often laden with frustration. For every one thing that worked, there were several problems that needed to be overcome. Without persistence, without dedication, nothing could have been accomplished. The pioneers featured in this book had the tenacity to find a way to bring their field forward.

# CHAPTER ONE

# James Marsh and Toxicology

Scientists have studied the effects of poisons for centuries. In 200 B.C., Niccander, the physician to a Middle Eastern king, conducted poison experiments. He tested the effects of poisons on human subjects—condemned criminals—and wrote an essay about poison antidotes. During the next two millennia, other individuals also tried to determine how poisons affect the body. Until the 1800s, however, when English chemist James Marsh appeared on the scene, scientists had made little progress in finding ways to prove that a poisoning had taken place.

Most people in the medical and legal professions held mistaken ideas about the characteristics of death by poisoning. For instance, normal attributes of a body's decay after death, such as having black or blue spots or a bad odor, were believed to be signs that the deceased had been poisoned. There was even a myth that the heart of a person who died of poisoning could not be burned by fire.

**antidote:** a substance that acts against the effects of a poison

*Chemist James Marsh (1794-1846) invented a device to detect arsenic poisoning, a popular method of murder during his lifetime.*

Dutch physician Hermann Boerhaave was the first person to offer a chemical-based method for detecting poisons. Around 1810, he stated that some poisons in a very hot or gaseous state have recognizable smells. Boerhaave thought that if substances suspected of containing poisons were heated on glowing coals, any poison in them would give off those particular smells.

Because death by poisoning was so difficult to prove, arsenic—a silvery, semimetallic element found in sulfide or metallic ores, such as copper and lead—was popular as a murder weapon until the twentieth century. Arsenic's notorious popularity was due to a number of factors.

First, an Arab chemist named Jabir discovered in the eighth century that arsenic could be converted into a white powder called arsenic oxide. This powder is commonly known as white arsenic. Tasteless and odorless, white arsenic could be added to the victim's food. The powder does not dissolve well in water, but it can be mixed into a thicker liquid well enough to hide its presence.

Second, because arsenic was commonly used to poison rats or kill weeds, it was easy to obtain. Third, not much arsenic is needed to kill someone (less than a quarter of a gram). Finally, the symptoms of arsenic poisoning—severe stomach cramps, vomiting, diarrhea—were similar to those of cholera. Spread by bacteria found in fecal-contaminated food or water, cholera was a common disease before modern sanitation. Accidental food poisoning was not particularly unusual either, so purposeful poisoning was difficult to prove in order to make a criminal case.

Members of legal systems in a number of countries often found it frustrating to try to prove death by arsenic poisoning and thought that many poisoners escaped detection. A number of people devised various methods of detecting the presence of poison, but none were completely reliable. For instance, in 1819, Samuel Farr suggested feeding the stomach contents of possible poisoning victims to animals to see if they became ill.

This was the situation in 1832, when English chemist James Marsh was called to investigate the suspected arsenic poisoning of George Bodle. James Marsh had been born on September 2, 1794. Little is known of his early life, except that he did well enough in his chemistry studies to become a chemist with the Royal Arsenal in Woolwich by 1822. In April 1823, the Society of Arts awarded Marsh its Large Silver Medal and 30 guineas in honor of a portable electromagnetic apparatus he invented.

**electromagnetism:** forces of attraction and repulsion produced by an electric current

In December 1829, while continuing to work for the Royal Arsenal, Marsh also became an assistant to scientist Michael Faraday at the Royal Military Academy. Faraday lectured on chemistry there. At the time of the Bodle death in Plumstead, near Woolwich, Marsh was working on a recoil brake for naval guns. As there was no other suitably educated chemist available in the area, Marsh reluctantly agreed to put his work aside to test the alleged victim, George Bodle, for arsenic poisoning.

*Scientist Michael Faraday (1791-1867) was known for his work with electricity, magnetism, and chemistry.*

Eighty-year-old George Bodle had been the grandfather of John Bodle. Rumor said that young John Bodle had grown impatient with waiting to inherit the farm from his overbearing grandfather. A local pharmacist told the police that he had twice sold John Bodle arsenic rat poison. A maid in the Bodle house reported that John had displayed uncharacteristically helpful behavior on the morning of his grandfather's illness by offering to bring water from the well for coffee.

The police had established that John Bodle had motive and opportunity, but that would not be enough to convict him of killing his grandfather. They needed physical proof. The police had wisely sealed the coffeepot and sent Bodle's body to a surgeon for an autopsy. Then they called in James Marsh to test the coffee and the deceased's intestines for the presence of arsenic.

Marsh researched the contemporary arsenic detection tests to find something he could use. He chose one in which stomach contents were mixed with hydrochloric acid and hydrogen sulfide. If arsenic was present in the stomach contents, a yellow precipitate (a solid substance that separates from a solution) would form. Marsh ran the test on the Bodle evidence, and he determined that arsenic was present.

**hydrochloric acid:** a clear, highly acidic solution used in chemistry

**hydrogen sulfide:** a colorless, flammable, poisonous gas used in chemistry to detect or measure another substance

Marsh was able to persuade the coroner's jury that George Bodle was poisoned. John Bodle was charged with his murder. At the December 1832 trial, however, the jurors were skeptical about the yellow precipitate Marsh displayed. To be convinced, the jurors felt they needed to see the arsenic itself. Marsh was frustrated and disappointed when John Bodle was found not guilty.

A decade later, John Bodle admitted that he had murdered his grandfather. In the meantime, James Marsh had set out to invent a way that arsenic could be made visible to everyone.

*Chemist Karl Wilhelm Scheele (1742-1786) discovered a number of acids, gases, and elements in his short but productive career. His death may have been caused by his habit of tasting the new compounds he prepared.*

**sulfuric acid:** a highly corrosive, thick, oily liquid used to manufacture a variety of chemicals and products such as paints and explosives

**zinc:** a shiny, blue-white metallic element that can be shaped when heated

## THE BREAKTHROUGH

In his studies, Marsh became interested in the theories of Swedish chemist Karl Wilhelm Scheele. In 1775, Scheele had discovered that adding chlorine water to white arsenic would transform it into arsenic acid. The acid could then be turned into arsine—an extremely poisonous gas with the odor of garlic—by placing it in contact with metallic zinc.

Arsine could also be developed by mixing sulfuric or hydrochloric acid with a fluid containing arsenic, and then adding zinc. During this process, hydrogen is created in a chemical reaction. The hydrogen, mixed with the arsenic, produces arsine gas.

Arsine was a key component in the simple but effective arsenic detection apparatus Marsh constructed. Marsh used a U-shaped glass tube opened at one end and with a glass nozzle at the other end. He suspended zinc at the nozzle end. At the open end, he poured the fluid he was checking for arsenic, mixed with acid. There was a flame under the tube to heat the liquid.

When the liquid sample reached the zinc, arsine gas would form if arsenic was present. Even a tiny bit of arsenic would be enough to produce arsine. The gas would escape through the nozzle and be ignited. Marsh would hold a cold porcelain bowl next to the flame, and a metallic version of the arsenic would settle and form a black deposit on the porcelain. Because the black deposit was actually the arsenic itself, everyone could witness the presence of the poison in a test fluid. A later modification of the apparatus made it possible to approximately determine the quantity of arsenic.

Even though the apparatus itself was uncomplicated, the test turned out to be very sensitive. Marsh said that a thousandth of a milligram of arsenic added to the test fluid would create a positive result.

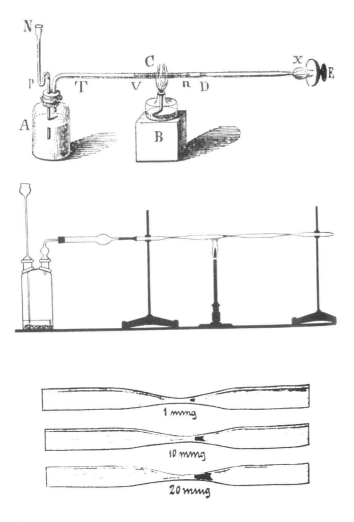

*The first apparatus invented by Marsh in 1836 (top), which he refined to measure the quantity of arsenic (center illustration). The bottom drawing shows how the arsenic was visibly measured in the device.*

This sensitivity made the test very reliable, but also added an unexpected twist in the coming years.

The *Edinburgh Philosophical Journal* printed Marsh's paper, "The Test for Arsenic," in October 1836, and it was subsequently translated into German and French (in 1842 and 1843 respectively). The Society of Arts awarded Marsh their Large Gold Medal for his invention. Marsh was also given a silver medal by the crown prince of Sweden in appreciation for his contributions to science.

Mathieu Orfila of Spain was among the first scientists to notice the new invention. In 1813, Orfila had published the first part of his two-volume work covering all the current knowledge about poisons. His books were well received by lawyers, police officials, and doctors across Europe. Orfila became known as the leading poison expert on the continent, but he had not been able to develop a test for detecting the presence of arsenic in a body. He put Marsh's test to use right away.

Orfila, as well as other chemists in France, made a discovery in 1838 that initially cast doubt on the dependability of the test's results. They found that the Marsh apparatus was making arsenic deposits even when the fluids did not have arsenic in them. After trying to figure out what was going wrong, they discovered that the sulfuric acid and zinc they were using contained arsenic.

The scientists concluded that before a test could be run, the testing agents themselves needed to be checked for arsenic. Marsh had actually pointed out in 1836 that his test was reliable as long as the zinc that was used did not have traces of arsenic in it. The full significance of his statement, however, was apparently not grasped immediately by his fellow scientists.

People used the Marsh apparatus to test many different things, even the ground under their feet. Scientists found that arsenic was present in some cemeteries, which made them worry that it might show up in bodies that had not been poisoned. Critics believed that finding arsenic in lots of places made the Marsh test more confusing than helpful. Orfila and others said that checking the soil around a body for arsenic and making sure the agents used in the test were arsenic-free would produce a reliable result from the Marsh apparatus.

In 1840, the field of toxicology and the Marsh apparatus caught the attention of the criminal justice system, as well as the public eye, with the Lafarge trial. Frenchwoman Marie Lafarge stood accused of poisoning her husband, Charles, with arsenic. Marsh's arsenic test was to play a pivotal role in the Lafarge case.

Five doctors from Brives, France, were responsible for testing the evidence for arsenic. They were unaware of the Marsh apparatus and used earlier methods, handled in a haphazard way, to run their tests. The Brives doctors determined that Charles Lafarge had died of arsenic poisoning.

"Fortunately, the investigation of poison murders has recently been revolutionized by advances in the science of chemistry" the state prosecutor said. "Probably the defendant would not stand before the

*Considered the founder of the field of toxicology, Mathieu Joseph Bonaventure Orfila (1787-1853) was born in Minorca and later worked in Paris.*

**toxicology:** the study of poisons—their effects, ways to detect them, and the treatments for poisoning

*Marie Lafarge testifying at her trial in 1840*

court right now had not science given us the means to prove the presence of poison where hitherto it could not be detected, in the very bodies of the victims." He was enthusiastic about the scientific evidence until the lawyer for the defense contacted Mathieu Orfila.

Orfila criticized the methods of the Brives doctors. He said that they were uninformed about poison detection because they were ignorant of the Marsh apparatus. The defense attorney wanted to bring Orfila to the court to run additional tests. The prosecution agreed to run new tests, but they wanted the tests to be done by local scientists, rather than by Orfila. The court had three scientists from Limoges conduct the tests.

The Limoges scientists used the Marsh apparatus and found no arsenic in the evidence. As only the stomach had been tested at this point, the prosecutor then asked for Charles Lafarge's other organs to be tested. Scientists from both Limoges and Brives worked together to examine the spleen, liver, lungs, heart, intestines, and brain. No arsenic was found in any of them. The prosecutor also asked that the remains of the beverages Lafarge had consumed (eggnog and sugar water) be tested, as well as some suspicious-looking powder Marie Lafarge possessed. Two members of the Limoges group inspected them and concluded there was arsenic in everything. They said the eggnog alone was poisonous enough to kill ten people.

Orfila was called in to clarify the situation. He ran tests himself, and arsenic was again found in the body. Orfila said that the Marsh apparatus was sensitive and that beginners, such as the Limoges scientists, could use it incorrectly. For instance, they could have had the flame under the test tube too hot, which would drive off the gas instead of allowing it to turn into a black deposit.

Marie Lafarge was found guilty of murdering her husband by poison. She was sentenced to life in prison with hard labor, although King Louis Phillippe later changed her sentence to life imprisonment without hard labor.

## THE RESULT

The Lafarge case left everyone talking, not only in France, but in all of Europe and the United States as well. The toxicology aspects of the case were central to people's interests. Could science prove beyond a shadow of a doubt that a person had been poisoned? Were the days of undetected poisonings over? What was next for toxicology?

In the twentieth century, toxicologists developed more advanced poison detection methods that replaced the Marsh test, such as X-ray fluorescence spectroscopy. The new methods are non-destructive, which means that the evidence that is being tested for poison is not destroyed during the testing process, as it is in the Marsh test.

Today, toxicologists can uncover many kinds of foreign substances in the body. In addition to testing for many types of poisons, they can detect the presence of drugs of all kinds—alcohol, narcotics, hallucinogens, painkillers, sports performance-enhancers—both in humans and animals. They are able to tell what quantity of a drug is present as well. Toxicologists also study the effects of exposure to chemicals on human health and on the environment.

Toxicology has advanced far from its humble beginnings. In a recent case in the United Kingdom in which a soldier was suspected of killing his wife by arsenic poisoning, the forensic scientists on the case were able to provide enough evidence for a conviction through analysis of the victim's hair. Their findings showed the presence of arsenic deposited at

**spectrometer:** an instrument that measures spectrums, such as the wavelengths of energy or the atomic and subatomic particles of a substance

**X-ray fluorescence spectrometer**: a spectrometer that uses X-rays and fluorescence (the emission of electromagnetic radiation) to separate the chemical parts of a substance so these elements can be identified and measured

intervals that coincided with her army husband's leave time.

Arsenic, long considered a "perfect weapon," was stripped of its cloak of anonymity by the persistent and clever chemist James Marsh. After the advent of the Marsh apparatus, murder by arsenic poisoning was likely to be uncovered. The field of toxicology advanced a huge step with the invention of the Marsh apparatus.

Marsh seems to have been devoted to science for science's sake, because he persisted in the face of financial hardship. He never earned more than 30 shillings a week and was said to have been depressed by his poverty. When he died on June 21, 1846, his widow was penniless, but the British government gave her an annual income of 20 pounds in recognition of her husband's work. The invention of the Marsh apparatus may not have made Marsh's fortune, but with it, James Marsh created a wealth of interest in toxicology that moved the field forward.

Dr. Alexander O. Gettler was the first toxicologist for New York City (1918). He examined tens of thousands of cadavers and found thousands of them had died of poisoning, including alcohol poisoning. Gettler measured how much alcohol by volume was present in the brain or spinal fluid to determine if a person had been intoxicated when he or she died.

# CHAPTER TWO

# Henry Faulds
# and Fingerprints

On the underside of each person's hands, there are tiny ridges in the skin, from the fingertips to the wrist. These ridges, which are also present on monkeys and other primates, have evolved for a threefold purpose. They increase touch sensitivity, help with gripping ability, and contain pores that allow the skin to perspire. An individual's ridges, plus the furrows in between, create patterns. These patterns are unique. No two people—not even identical twins—share the same patterns. When the ridges come in contact with objects, perspiration and natural body oils on the hand leave impressions of these patterns—fingerprints. These marks aren't usually visible to the naked eye, yet fingerprints are everywhere.

Although solving crimes through fingerprint identification is a relatively recent development, fingerprints have been used as personal identifiers for thousands of years. Even without conducting scientific studies to prove it, a number of groups and

*Many scientists studied fingerprints in the 1800s, but it was physician Henry Faulds (1843-1930) who first realized their potential in police work.*

individuals correctly guessed that their fingertips had special patterns.

In ancient China, traders used marks made by blackened thumbs as seals, and divorce contracts were signed with a handprint. People in Japan also have long used finger and hand marks as signatures; an ancient emperor's handprint was found in a Japanese temple in the city of Kyoto.

Western examples of this practice include a 1691 petition by 225 townspeople of Londonderry, Ireland. When asking the king of Britain for compensation for their wartime losses, the townspeople presented their request in a petition bearing their signatures. Each signature was accompanied by a fingerprint, to make the petition more official. Nearly a hundred years later, English author and engraver Thomas Beswick (1753-1828) used wooden carvings of his own fingerprints as his trademark and as a proof of authenticity.

The individuality of fingerprints makes them a boon to law enforcement, but there is another quality that is also essential—their unchangeability. Before fingerprints could become part of police procedure, someone had to realize that they do not change over the course of a person's life. That person was Scottish doctor Henry Faulds.

Henry was born in Beith, Ayrshire, on June 1, 1843. At age 12, he went to Glasgow to work for his uncle. Three years later he joined a dress and shawl manufacturing company and worked there for five years. "His experience with this firm in the arrangement and classification of shawl patterns had no little

Three or four months before babies are born, tiny ridges form on their fingers, toes, hands, and feet. These ridges will grow with the child, but the unique pattern will never change.

bearing upon . . . the making of his great discovery," said biographer George Wilton Wilton.

During this time, Faulds took private classes to prepare for the University of Glasgow, which he attended from 1864 to 1867. He then studied medicine at Anderson's College in Glasgow, becoming a licensed physician in 1871. Strongly religious, Faulds wanted to be a medical missionary. The young doctor spent most of 1872 and half of 1873 working in India before a conflict with the head of the mission sent him back to Scotland. While home that summer, he married Isabella Wilson and applied for mission work. In December 1873, at age 30, Faulds left his Scotland home to become a medical missionary in Japan.

Faulds found the situation in Japan more to his liking than his post in India and established a hospital in Tsuki, near Tokyo. Within a couple of years, the hospital was treating 9,000 patients a year. In addition to his work as the hospital superintendent, Faulds also started a medical journal. At the same time, he helped publish a raised-letter Bible for the blind.

The Japanese were very fond of Henry Faulds. In 1875, he was offered a position as a Japanese prince's personal physician. As the post would have required him to abandon his missionary work, Faulds said no. A year later, he set up a medical school at the mission.

One day in 1878, while he was walking on the beach, Faulds came upon pieces of pottery that had been baked in the sun. He noticed the preserved impressions of the potter's fingertips. He then began to give a lot of thought to fingerprints. At first he wondered what could be learned from fingerprints. Was it possible to tell a person's race from prints? Could patterns be inherited?

Faulds observed thousands of fingers directly, by bringing his students, patients, and fellow medical personnel into his studies. Then he examined finger impressions on various substances, such as putty, clay, and beeswax. During the course of his investigations, Faulds began thinking of ways fingerprints might be useful.

The forensic use of fingerprints became clear to Henry Faulds when he was told about a sooty print a thief had left on a wall near Faulds's home. He compared the print with that of an arrested suspect and found that they did not match. Faulds told the police that the suspect was innocent. A few days later, another suspect was captured. Faulds compared this new suspect's prints with those on the wall. They were the same, and the suspect confessed.

On a second occasion, the Japanese police came to Faulds for help with an unsolved crime. The prints Faulds found on a mug at the scene of the crime matched a set that he had taken in the course of his fingerprint studies. The prints belonged to a servant who, when confronted, admitted he was guilty.

**plastic fingerprints:** impressions of fingerprints left in a soft substance such as paint, wax, or chocolate

**visible (or patent) fingerprints:** fingerprints easily seen by the human eye. Someone with dirt, blood, or grease on his or her fingers would leave visible prints.

# THE BREAKTHROUGH

With the help of his Japanese students, Faulds conducted tests to see if fingerprints could be changed. They first shaved off the ridges from their own hands, to see if the patterns would grow back exactly the same way. They did. Faulds wrote, "Then we used pumice stone, sand-paper, emery-dust, various acids, caustics, and even Spanish fly" to ensure that precisely the same patterns would arise, no matter how they were removed.

Faulds made observations not only during planned tests, but also under spontaneous conditions. When an outbreak of scarlet fever struck, he studied the fingertips of his patients. The fever sometimes caused the skin to peel off their fingertips, but the new skin that grew had the same pattern as the old. Faulds became convinced that a person's fingerprints did not change.

By 1880, Faulds was ready to share his findings with others. He prepared outlines of hands, with directions for making a print. In February, he wrote to scientist Charles Darwin and asked for help with his fingerprint studies. Darwin, famous for his idea that living things evolve over time, wrote back in April, telling Faulds that he was not in a position to help because he was in poor health. Darwin said he would pass the letter along to his cousin, Francis Galton, who was also a scientist and might be able to assist Faulds. Historians believe that Darwin did forward the letter to Galton—it was not found among Darwin's papers—but Galton never contacted Faulds.

**caustics:** substances capable of burning, corroding, or dissolving by chemical action

**Spanish fly:** a green beetle that can be dried and crushed to create a toxic preparation used as an irritant

*Charles Darwin (1809-1882) as he looked about the time Faulds wrote to him*

*Francis Galton (1822-1911) studied several areas of science, but concentrated on human heredity.*

Scientists studying the evolution of the human race have concluded that fingerprints are one to two million years old!

Faulds also wrote to others in 1880 about his studies. He sent letters to Scotland Yard in London and to the police in Paris to recommend the use of fingerprints to catch criminals. Both agencies were resistant to such a new idea.

In their October 28, 1880, issue, the science journal *Nature* published a letter by Faulds discussing his thoughts on the usefulness of fingerprints. He announced his conviction that "when bloody finger marks or impressions on clay, glass, etc. exist, they may lead to the scientific identification of criminals." He mentioned the two Japanese cases in which his knowledge of fingerprints had led to arrests.

In addition to fingerprints left at the scene of a crime, Faulds referred to other occasions in which fingerprints might solve a case. He gave the famous Tichborne case as an example. In 1854, Lord James Tichborne's eldest son, Roger, had been lost at sea. Eleven years later, a man living in Australia said he was Roger and claimed the large inheritance. Many family members believed him, but several years later, the Tichborne Claimant, as he was known, lost his case in court. He had been caught lying during the trial and was imprisoned for 10 years for perjury (giving false information to a court). Faulds thought fingerprints could have conclusively resolved that case.

*The issue of* Nature *magazine in which Faulds's letter appeared in 1880*

Faulds also suggested the creation of a register of criminals' fingerprints: "There can be no doubt as to the advantage of having, besides their photographs, a nature-copy of the forever-unchangeable finger-furrows of important criminals." He described the equipment needed to make a print, and even how to remove the ink from hands afterwards, saying, "A little hot water and soap remove the ink. Benzine is still more effective." Eager to get the ball rolling, he stated, "I have had prepared a number of outline hands with blank forms for entering such particulars of each case as may be wanted. . . . Each fingertip may best be done singly."

After the letter to *Nature* was published, Faulds received letters from around the world from scientists and others interested in his work. In November 1880, *Nature* printed a letter from William Herschel (1833-1917) responding to Faulds's letter. Herschel, a civil servant in India, stated that in his work, he had been taking fingerprints for 20 years. Part of his job was to distribute pensions. Many of the recipients could not read or write, so Herschel used fingerprints to prevent one person from pretending to be another. Herschel also used fingerprints as signatures on contracts. He observed that these "signatures" remained the same even as a person aged and concluded that fingerprints don't change over time. Although Herschel didn't mention anything about using fingerprints found at the scene of a crime to identify the culprit, this letter would prove to be significant to Faulds's later life and work.

# THE RESULT

Faulds continued his mission work and his studies in Japan for five more years, leaving there at the end of 1885 because his wife, Isabella, was ill. They lived in London for a few years. Faulds took this opportunity to go to the British Museum to check on his theory that the fingertip patterns on Egyptian mummies might be intact enough to be studied (he had also mentioned that possibility in his letter to *Nature*). He found that the mummies did indeed still have fingerprints.

Henry Faulds also visited Scotland Yard to convince them to use fingerprints as a crime-solving tool. He even offered "to work a small bureau, free of expense, in order to test its value and practicability." Officials thought him a nuisance, however, and one said that no one could be convicted based "on identification of features confined within so small a space as a . . . tip of a finger." Faulds invited Inspector John Tunbridge to his home one afternoon to show him his ideas. Tunbridge was sympathetic to Faulds, but didn't think his ideas could really be put into practice. (Two decades later, however, Tunbridge wrote Faulds to tell him that as commissioner of police in New Zealand, he had introduced fingerprinting into their system.)

In 1888, Francis Galton was preparing a lecture on Bertillonage (the method of using extensive facial and body measurements for identification devised by Alphonse Bertillon in 1879) and wrote to the editors of *Nature* asking for information about

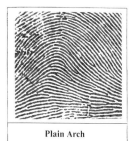

**Plain Arch**

**Loop**

**Whorl**

*Fingerprints are organized into three main types of patterns. Arches have ridges that run from one side of the finger to the other, loops make a backward turn, and whorls have ridges that make a circle. Some people's fingerprints include elements of all three patterns and are called composites.*

fingerprints. In a twist of fate, the editors sent Herschel's address to Galton, but not Faulds's. Perhaps they did not have it because he had left Japan. For whatever reason, this small mistake may have been responsible for Galton giving Herschel credit for Faulds's idea. Galton wrote to Herschel, who happily sent Galton all of his information on fingerprinting and visited Galton, as well, to show his technique.

Galton published his first book on fingerprints in 1892. Many people were interested in his description of the details of finger ridges, which are still sometimes referred to as "Galton's Details" or "Galton's Ridges." In the book, Galton acknowledged a large debt to Herschel, and in his one dismissive reference to Faulds misspelled his name. In another published reference to Faulds, Galton mistakenly said that Herschel's letter in *Nature* was published before Faulds's. Herschel did nothing to correct the record until late in his life. Meanwhile, the views of Herschel and Galton—well-esteemed men, both of whom were knighted during their lifetimes—were accepted by most people.

In 1891, after reading Galton's book, an innovative Argentine police official named Juan Vucetich (1858-1925) built a fingerprint office at his own expense and came up with a print classification system that continues to be used in South America. The following year, he made an arrest in a double murder case based on fingerprint evidence. Word of Vucetich's success, however, did not reach Europe or the United States.

*Mark Twain's fiction anticipated fact. In 1883, when using fingerprints for identification was unheard of in America and just beginning to be discussed elsewhere, Twain's book* Life on the Mississippi *included the chapter, "A thumb-print and what came of it." Twain returned to this theme in 1894 in his story* Pudd'nhead Wilson. *A lawyer, Wilson uses fingerprints to track down a murderer and declares in court that no one can disguise his or her fingerprints.*

That same year, Faulds became a police surgeon, which he would remain for eight years before starting a private practice. In 1901—20 years after Faulds initially suggested it—England and Wales finally started using fingerprints for criminal identification. The method of categorizing the prints that they adopted was created by Edward Henry (1850-1931), who later was knighted for his contributions to law enforcement.

There was some question about who really made the Henry System—Henry or some of his

*A caricature of Edward Henry that appeared in* Vanity Fair *in 1905*

Indian employees, especially a man named Khan Azizul Haque. Although in 1900 Henry claimed that the system was his alone, 26 years later he wrote that Haque "contributed more than any other member of my staff and contributed in a conspicuous degree" to making the system. Regardless, the system, still in use today, is known as the Henry classification system.

In 1902, the feelings of the British government toward Faulds thawed a bit. He was asked to give evidence for a committee considering the use of fingerprints to catch army deserters. Some officials told him that he would be given a job in the Scotland fingerprinting office, if one was established there. This never happened, but after being dismissed as a fraud for years, Faulds welcomed the recognition.

Faulds's career still had some bumps. When he published a *Guide to Fingerprint Identification* in 1905, Galton was the one who reviewed the book for *Nature*. Galton gave it a negative review, writing, "His book is not only biased and imperfect, but unfortunately it contains nothing new that is of value." That same year, Faulds attended the first British trial where fingerprints were given as evidence. Faulds's animosity toward Scotland Yard was so deep, due to their past rejections of his ideas, that he sided against the fingerprint evidence, stating that not enough details matched for the prints to be the same. Nevertheless, Scotland Yard won the case.

Herschel published *The Origin of Finger-Printing* in 1916, completely omitting Faulds. In 1917, the year Herschel died, he acknowledged that

Faulds's idea to use fingerprints to identify criminals was "a conception so different from mine." Galton had already died, six years earlier, and so never saw his friend's admission.

Despite his frustrations, Faulds continued studying fingerprints. He edited the fingerprint journal *Dactylography* in the early 1920s and published a book called *Manual of Practical Dactylography* in 1923. Faulds died on March 19, 1930. The Japanese erected a commemorative stone in his honor in Tokyo identifying him as a "pioneer in fingerprint identification."

Since Faulds's time, fingerprints have turned out to be a significant, if challenging, tool for law enforcement. Some of the greatest challenges that have faced modern fingerprint experts are the detection and development of latent fingerprints. Latent fingerprints are ones that have been left at the scene of a crime but are not visible. On the other hand, visible, or patent, fingerprints are easily seen by the human eye. Someone with dirt, blood, or grease on his or her fingers would leave visible prints.

More than a hundred different ways of making latent prints visible have been invented. The earliest and most popular methods use powder and brushes, but other, more recent, techniques employ chemicals, lasers, Super Glue, and even lifting prints with transparent tape.

In the 1980s, computers revolutionized the way in which fingerprint records are kept and compared today. Using the Automated Fingerprint Identification System (AFIS), a scanner can convert a

**dactylography:** the study of fingerprints as a method of identification

*Prints deliberately taken from an individual by inking each finger and then pressing them onto a white card are called rolled fingerprints.*

person's prints into digital data. Millions of fingerprints can be stored in one database. When the police have prints they wish to identify, the AFIS program can quickly locate any prints that come close to those in question. A fingerprint expert then examines the possibilities for a match.

The experience of the San Francisco police department illustrates the power of the AFIS. In 1983, using only visual comparisons by experts, the police were able to resolve 58 cases involving latent fingerprints found at crime scenes. In 1984, after installing the computer system, the police cleared 816 latent-print cases, including 52 homicides.

Fingerprint identification has made great strides since Henry Faulds's initial conception of it, and recognition of Faulds has made progress as well. In 1987, two American fingerprint experts paid for a plaque to be added to the Faulds family gravesite in recognition of his work.

*An Automated Fingerprint Identification System (AFIS) being used to compare fingerprints*

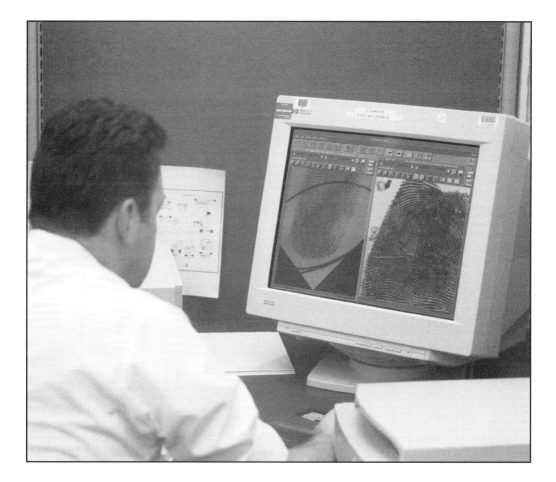

# CHAPTER THREE

# Albert Sherman Osborn and Questioned Documents

Every literate culture—one that communicates using words on paper—has had to fight forgery. Criminals have faked or altered wills, contracts, deeds, and other important documents since ancient times. As far back as A.D. 539, the crime of forgery was such a problem that Roman law stated that experts were needed to compare handwriting to judge document authenticity.

No one knows how many forged documents were accepted as authentic when few people knew how to read and write. The actions of aristocrats and other people of the educated elite were often considered beyond question. As the number of literate people has increased and the equipment for writing and printing has advanced, forgery has evolved, too. With the invention of typewriters and, later, computers, fraudulent documents have created different challenges for the specialists known as questioned-document examiners.

*Albert Sherman Osborn (1858-1946) pioneered a scientific approach not only to analyze handwriting, but also in examining ink, paper, and printing in order to authenticate a document.*

*Algernon Sidney (1622-1683) is best remembered for his book* Discourses Concerning Government, *a manuscript copy of which was used as evidence against him during his trial.*

Another challenge that has faced questioned-document examiners is that their field was often not accepted. After the Algernon Sidney case in 1683, for example, British courts did not allow evidence about handwriting on the grounds that handwriting could not be identified as belonging to a certain person. In this case, a document introduced as evidence had convinced a jury to find philosopher and political activist Algernon Sidney guilty of treason. The document, a book found in Sidney's closet, was reported to have his writing in it—but no witnesses testified to that. Some witnesses said in court that the writing was similar to what they had seen Sidney write 20 years or so before. Based on this dubious evidence, Sidney was executed as a traitor. But in 1689, an Act of Parliament overturned Sidney's conviction because the treasonous writing was not adequately proved to be written by him.

Handwriting comparison was again allowed in British civil cases in 1854 and in criminal cases in 1865. Although those changes occurred in the nineteenth century, document examination as a field was developed primarily in the twentieth century.

The dedicated expert who would turn things around in American document examination was Albert Sherman Osborn. Born in 1858 to William and Jane Cole Osborn, Albert was the second of the couple's six children. The Osborn family lived on a farm in Grass Lake, Michigan, where Albert helped with the farm work. He went to the nearby country school, but he wanted to go away to college to learn something other than farming.

When Osborn attended college in Lansing, Michigan, penmanship—the art of handwriting—caught his interest. Hoping that if he worked hard enough at it, he could become a penmanship teacher, Osborn practiced determinedly. His efforts made him a highly skilled penman.

In a frightening turn of events, Osborn came down with an eye illness that could have ended his career before it started. He went home to his parents' farm in Grass Lake to recover. Perhaps the change of scenery was what he needed. Within a year, his illness had disappeared.

One day in 1882, after putting in a hard day's work plowing the fields, Osborn found a letter from the Rochester Business Institute waiting for him. The school offered Osborn a job as a penmanship teacher. He jumped at the opportunity and informed his family that he had plowed his last field.

Prior to the introduction of mass-produced fountain pens in the 1880s and ballpoint pens in 1944, people used pens made of such materials as reeds, bamboo, rushes, or feather quills.

*Albert Osborn as he looked while teaching at the Rochester Business Institute*

Once Osborn was settled in Rochester, New York, he also became interested in questioned document issues—the identification of handwriting, paper, inks, typewriting, and so on. As there were no questioned document experts at that time, lawyers would bring their questions about suspicious-looking documents to penmanship teachers. Once Osborn's skills in his profession became known, lawyers started asking him about their document dilemmas.

To determine if handwriting on a document is genuine, the examiner looks at the shape and size of the letters, their spacing, and the way the curves, loops, upstrokes, and downstrokes are made. An expert can also spot if a writer has retraced letters or hesitated while writing.

Forgeries are usually written much more slowly than regular signatures and have frequent changes of the grasp of the pencil or pen, poor line quality, retraces and patches, and starts and stops. In other words, the letters may have the right shape, but they are not written with the rapid ease that a person develops after years of signing the same name.

Although Osborn firmly believed that expert document examination could play an important role in aiding the cause of justice, he faced a hard road convincing the legal profession. At that time, any kind of expert evidence was judged harshly in courts. Lawyers were known for hiring experts who would make claims that supported whichever side of the case paid their fee.

The way a person writes numbers can be identified in the same basic way that handwriting can.

People write their own names a little differently every time.

Since the quality of work from some document examiners was not very scientific, the courts had good reason to be wary. In the late 1800s, many "handwriting experts" used only an ordinary reading glass for magnification and did not work full time in the field. But the rules faced by those experts who wanted to act professionally often prevented them from providing useful evidence.

For example, experts could not show documents containing handwriting known to belong to a person for comparison with handwriting on a questioned document, unless those identified documents were used as evidence for some other reason. How could a jury decide whether handwriting was forged if they couldn't see what a person's usual handwriting looked like?

Tools such as magnifying glasses, microscopes, and enlarged photographs of the handwriting were sometimes not allowed in court, which kept a jury from having a good look at the writing in question. But perhaps worst of all was the rule stating that experts could not explain their conclusions. Without hearing an expert's reasons, how could a jury or judge know whether the expert had used a scientific method or had just been paid to state a certain opinion? How could anyone decide if an expert's deductions were sound and convincing?

Objections to the use of the microscope in court are based upon the . . . erroneous idea that what exists that is significant can be seen by unaided vision. Ordinary spectacles are simply lenses placed between the eye and the object looked at, by which means sight is corrected and improved, and the most elaborate and complicated microscope is nothing more than an extension of this principle. To be consistent, one who objects to the use of the microscope should also insist that judge and jury should be compelled to remove spectacles before examining a document.
—Albert S. Osborn

## THE BREAKTHROUGH

In December 1898, Harry S. Cornish, the athletic director at the exclusive Knickerbocker Athletic Club in New York City, received an anonymous package. Presumably a Christmas present, it contained a silver bottle holder with a container of Bromo Seltzer powder that fit neatly into the holder. He thought the medicine, used to relieve headaches and stomachaches, was a practical joke and took the package home. The next day his aunt, Katherine Adams, with whom Cornish lived, drank some of the seltzer mixed in water and died half an hour later. An autopsy revealed she had been poisoned with cyanide of mercury; an analysis of the "seltzer" confirmed it to be cyanide. Cornish, who had tasted the mixture when his aunt complained of the bitter taste, had become ill. When he recovered, he gave the package that the "gift" had arrived in to the police.

Ten handwriting experts, including Osborn, were asked to identify the person who had written Cornish's address on the package. They concluded that the writing implicated Roland Molineux, a wealthy member of the Knickerbocker who had argued with Cornish about club policies many times. The district attorney was so convinced by their conclusions that, despite Molineux's social position, he charged Molineux with the crime. During the trial, the experts' testimonies were thoughtfully presented and included photographic enlargements to illustrate their points. The jury found Molineux guilty . . . but that wasn't the end of the story.

On appeal, Molineux was granted a new trial in 1902 with a new judge, who made unfavorable comments about the experts' evidence to the jury and did not let the experts present their photographs. The attitude of this new judge disturbed Osborn, and so did the verdict—the jury found Molineux not guilty.

Osborn had similar experiences with other cases in which document-examination experts were not given a fair chance in court. Frustrated but determined, Osborn decided to try to change the

*The police also suspected Roland Molineux of poisoning a rival for the affections of his wife, Blanche, before their marriage. He was never charged, but Blanche left her husband after his second trial.*

situation. He knew that lawyers and judges needed to understand what document examination was and how its evidence could best be explained in court. The qualifications for being a document examiner had to improve as well.

Osborn's first step was to write articles for legal publications on the subject of questioned documents. He also researched issues dealing with paper and inks, as well as whether typewriting could be identified as having come from a certain make of typewriter or from a certain machine. Up until this point, people had assumed that typewriting could not be identified. Osborn, however, soon concluded that this was possible.

Osborn discovered that a typewriter's make and model can be identified based on the style of type, its size, and the spacing between the letters. This identification of make and model narrows down the possibilities of which typewriter may have been used to produce a document, but cannot pinpoint the actual machine. Once they have been used, however, typewriters can develop flaws that make them different from even others of the same style made by the same company. For example, a little bit of a certain letter may be missing. These flaws can sometimes be used to identify a specific typewriting machine. Typewriter ribbons have also provided evidence, because in some cases it is possible to read what has been typed by looking at the marks left on a particular ribbon.

Osborn's typewriting work was put to the test in 1908 in an important government case. President

Paper was probably invented about A.D. 105 in China, where it was made from a mixture of bark and hemp. Before the fifteenth century, when paper became widespread in Europe, documents were written on parchment, which was made from specially prepared cow or sheep skin. Today's paper is prepared from cellulose pulp obtained from wood.

Theodore Roosevelt's administration disagreed with Congress about the number of battleships versus submarines they should plan to make. In the course of their dispute, it became crucial to identify the writer of some anonymous typewritten papers. Osborn, now a well-known examiner of questioned documents, provided key testimony regarding the origin of these papers.

In 1910, Osborn left the Rochester Business Institute to go to New York City to open his own questioned-document examination office. He was handling enough business in questioned documents that he felt he could focus his energies on it full time. Osborn was right about the need for an office such as his—he received cases from across the United States and from every province in Canada, as well as from other countries.

To fill the need for better equipment for document inspection, Osborn designed and constructed a number of glass instruments. These tools took tiny width, height, and angle measurements. Because they were made of glass, they allowed the examiner to place the device directly onto the document and still read the writing underneath.

The same year that Osborn started his office in New York City, he published a book that would become the classic in his field, *Questioned Documents*. This work helped document examination become accepted by the legal world. In *Questioned Documents*, Osborn took a scientific approach, giving thoughtful, understandable reasons for his conclusions.

*Albert S. Osborn and his wife, Elizabeth, had three children: Dorothy, Paul G., who was killed in France in 1917, and Albert D., pictured here, who joined his father's questioned-document business in 1919.*

Osborn also named his own occupation when he introduced the term "examiner of questioned documents." He explained that "handwriting expert," which was the usual term, left out too many other document-related issues, such as paper, ink, and typewriting. Although handwriting is a significant part of their work, examiners of questioned documents must have a broad range of knowledge and also know where to turn for expert opinions about topics that are not their specialties. For example, examiners may turn to chemists for information about the age of an ink.

## THE RESULT

Document examination was an accepted forensic field when Albert S. Osborn was called upon to testify regarding the ransom notes in the famous Lindbergh kidnapping case. Charles Lindbergh, a wildly popular figure of the time, had piloted the first solo airplane flight across the Atlantic Ocean in 1927. Five years later, the baby son of Charles and his wife, Anne Morrow Lindbergh, was kidnapped.

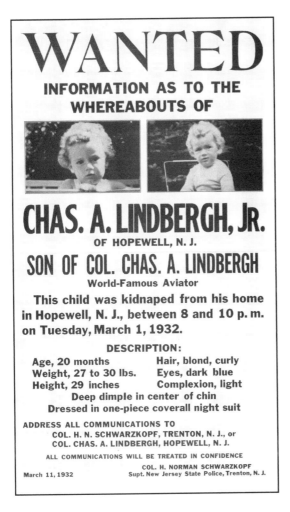

*This plea for help in the Lindbergh kidnapping case remains poignant years after the event.*

In a handwritten note, the kidnapper demanded $50,000. The Lindberghs received a total of 15 messages with instructions and demands before the body of their little son, who had been murdered, was found near their home.

Osborn and seven other document examiners studied the ransom notes as well as hundreds of samples of suspects' handwriting to ascertain the author.

*The original ransom note, left in the Lindberghs' home. It reads: "Dear Sir: Have 50.000$ redy 25000$ in 20$ bills 15000$ in 10$ bills and 10000$ in 5$ bills. After 2-4 days we will inform you were to deliver the mony. We warn you for making anyding public or for notify the Police. The child is in gute care. Indication for all letters are Signature and 3 holes." All 15 notes contained this symbol of the 3 holes, as well as some of the same spelling and grammatical errors.*

*Albert D. Osborn prepares to testify about the analysis he and his father made of the ransom notes in the Lindbergh case.*

Osborn, his son and partner, Albert D. Osborn, and the other examiners identified Bruno Richard Hauptmann, who was found guilty of the murder and executed in 1936.

Now accepted in the legal world, document examiners have had to scramble to keep up with new technology such as computer printers and photocopiers. Ways to trace documents to these new tools have been found, however, just as Osborn learned to work with the typewriter. The paper of a document may have marks from the belts, rollers, and gears that move it through the machine. The toners used in some printers and copiers consist of different chemicals. Toner can sometimes clump together in detectable patterns. The glass portions of photocopiers can have scratches that leave identifiable marks.

Questioned-document cases now cover a wide scope of topics. They include investigation of credit-card slips, robbery "hold-up" notes, business records, anonymous letters, computer printouts, lottery tickets, insurance forms, medical records, and counterfeit money.

Making money that counterfeiters cannot duplicate has always provided governments with a formidable task. The U.S. government, for example, changed its currency in the late 1990s by adding color-shifting inks, a watermark, an off-center presidential portrait, and micro-printing. Micro-printing—extremely small lettering that looks like a thin line to the naked eye—is useful because it looks blurry when it is copied, so counterfeiters cannot create a clear image by using a top-of-the-line copier or printer.

Other companies, such as credit-card makers, also face clever counterfeiters. The holograms—three-dimensional images—VISA placed on its credit cards were intended to stop counterfeiters in their tracks. In less than a month, however, fake VISAs with holograms were available. The work to recognize forgeries and to foil forgers never ends.

Although there are huge numbers of questions that document examiners may be called upon to answer, questions about handwriting remain among those most often asked. Questioned-document examiner Emily Will explained that people usually want to know one of the following things:

Is this signature genuine?

Out of this group of people, who wrote this anonymous letter?

Did someone guide this person's hand as the document was signed?

Did the signer of the document also initial the changes?

What is written under the crossed-out portion of the writing?

To answer questions about writing that has been erased or crossed out, document examiners may use infrared and ultraviolet photography. They can also use chemical treatments that don't damage the document.

These advances in questioned document technology would have certainly pleased Osborn, who devoted his whole life to the field. As well as creating document analysis devices and writing *Questioned Documents*, Osborn wrote *The Problem of Proof* (1922), *The Mind of the Juror* (1937), and *Questioned Document Problems* (1944). In 1942, the American Society of Questioned Document Examiners was formed, with Osborn as its first president. He held this post until he died in 1946.

*Albert S. Osborn wrote some of the first books about questioned documents. They are part of his descendants' library of over 1,400 books and articles on document examination and related forensic sciences.*

Roscoe Pound, Dean of Harvard University's Law School, wrote in 1944, "It is not too much to say that [Osborn] has created the profession of examiner of questioned documents in this country and has turned what had been largely a matter of superficial guesswork or plausible advocacy into a matter of scientific investigation and demonstration."

Osborn's son, Albert D., grandson Paul A., and great-grandson John Paul all carried on the practice that Albert Sherman founded. In 2001, Paul and John Paul Osborn, forensic document examiners, continued to operate the four-generation family practice from their office and laboratory in Union, New Jersey.

John Paul Osborn, Albert's great-grandson, carries on the family business with the latest equipment in the field. The Osborns' laboratory includes a computer and imaging equipment (top left) and a camera copy stand (top right) with a Video Spectral Comparator (VSC) used to differentiate inks and examine obliterated writing.

# CHAPTER FOUR

# Charles Waite and Calvin Goddard and Firearm Examination

Forensic specialists who study guns and ammunition are known as ballistic experts or firearm examiners. When guns are involved in a crime, firearm experts try to uncover all the gun-related information they can that might help solve the crime. They note the gun's model, caliber, and serial number, and examine it for fingerprints, blood, hair, or other substances. If there are bullets that have been shot, firearm examiners may be able to match the bullets to a suspect's gun. They can sometimes determine when a gun was last fired or how far away the shooter was from the victim.

Small arms or handguns were first generally used in the late 1300s. They resembled a small cannon and had to be lit with a match to fire. By the late 1500s, guns such as muskets or pistols were in use. These guns were loaded by pouring gunpowder into the barrel muzzle, then dropping a lead ball down the barrel. A paper wad was also put into the

**ballistics:** the study of thrown or propelled objects in flight. The term can apply to the travel paths of spacecraft or large missiles, but in forensics the term refers to bullets and the guns that fire them.

*Although trained as a doctor, Calvin Goddard (1891-1955) was more interested in guns. He joined detective Charles Waite to establish the first ballistics laboratory in the United States.*

**pistol:** a firearm designed to be held and fired with one hand

**gunsmith:** a person who makes or repairs firearms

*This Colt Single Action Army Model 1873—called the gun that "won the West"— held six shots in its revolving cylinder.*

barrel to keep the ball and powder from moving. Then the entire load was packed down with a long, thin rod called a ramrod. The barrel of the gun was completely smooth and bullets generally were loose inside. In the 1800s, revolvers that held up to six bullets in a cylinder replaced the tedious barrel-loading guns. Bullets were packed in cartridges that also contained the explosive powder to fire the bullets. Automatic-firing weapons were developed in the early 1900s.

It was the invention of the rifle in the 1400s, however, that was a breakthrough for both gun users and, later, forensics. Gunsmiths added spiral grooves on the inside of the gun barrel—known as rifling—that made bullets in flight rotate. This process of rifling made guns more accurate and able to shoot

farther. Rifling also produced tiny imperfections on the inside of the gun barrel. These flaws differ from gun to gun, even if the weapons are made with the same tools. When a bullet is fired, the imperfections leave individualized marks on the bullet. Today, all types of guns except shotguns are rifled.

In 1889, Professor Alexandre Lacassagne of Lyons University in France observed these rifling marks on a bullet used in a murder. He began studying the suspects' revolvers and discovered that only one had a barrel with seven grooves, the same number of grooves that were on the bullet. The owner of the seven-grooved gun was convicted in one of the first decisions based on ballistics evidence. Firearm experts today would not consider that alone enough proof to decide a case. Contemporary firearm examiners have more resources and precise tools and tests than those available to Lacassagne, thanks in part to detective Charles E. Waite.

In 1917, Charles Waite, a middle-aged investigator in the New York State attorney general's office, was part of an independent commission assigned to review the Charles Stielow murder case. Waite had long been drawn to crime-solving, but had not found his niche yet. He had led, in the words of historian Jurgen Thorwald, "a variegated and on the whole unproductive life."

The Stielow case, which would give a focus to Waite's life, began in 1915 in Orleans County, New York. Charles Stielow, a farm laborer, was accused of murdering his employer, Charles Phelps, and Margaret Wolcott, Phelps's housekeeper. The only

Alexandre Lacassagne was a pathologist who developed techniques for identifying human remains. His work was well known, and the police often called upon him for assistance.

evidence against Stielow was that of self-proclaimed ballistics expert Albert Hamilton, who said the bullets used in the murders had come from Stielow's gun. On July 23, 1915, the jury found Stielow guilty and sentenced him to death.

A deputy warden, who thought Stielow might be innocent, contacted a humanitarian group on his behalf. They hired private detectives who discovered that two drifters, now in prison, had been overheard discussing the murders. A member of the humanitarian group, attorney Grace Humiston, obtained a confession from one of these convicts. The prisoner later changed his mind about his confession, but enough questions about Stielow's guilt were raised that the governor of New York arranged for investigators George Bond and Charles Waite to look into the matter.

Waite took the bullets used in the murder and Stielow's gun to a New York City police detective. The detective compared bullets fired from the gun to the murder bullets and found that they had important differences. The bullets from the murder scene had an unusually wide land (space between grooves), whereas the test bullets did not. Bond and Waite concluded that Stielow's gun did not fire the bullets that killed Wolcott and Phelps. The governor of New York pardoned Stielow, who had already spent three years in prison and had been minutes away from dying in the electric chair on one occasion. The prisoner who had earlier confessed to the murders and then recanted now confessed once again. Although Waite and others believed he and the other

**land:** the raised portion of a grooved surface

drifter were guilty, the Grand Jury of Orleans County refused to indict either man for murder, probably to save the legal costs of another trial.

This injustice preyed on Waite's mind. He wanted to take action to prevent it from happening again. He thought that if people in the legal system knew more about guns—and the ways they are distinct from each other—mistakes in firearm identification could be avoided. Waite was sidetracked by World War I, but after the war was over in 1918, he got to work. His goal: to collect information about all the firearms ever made in America.

*Identifying lands and grooves are visible on this spent bullet.*

caliber: the diameter of the inside of the barrel of a firearm, usually measured in hundredths or thousandths of an inch and written as a decimal fraction, such as .45 caliber

## THE BREAKTHROUGH

Waite traveled the country gathering details of gun construction, types of ammunition, the proportion of grooves to lands, calibers, groove twists, and anything else he could think of. He went directly to the factories where the guns were made, spoke to the managers, and pored over old notebooks filled with gun measurements. As Waite intended to accumulate information about every American gun produced since the 1850s, his project was not a quick one. But by 1922, he had done it. In his search, Waite found that his hypothesis was correct—no type of gun was exactly like any other.

Before Waite even had a chance to enjoy his success, he discovered he had more work to do. About two-thirds of the guns in the United States at that time had come from Europe. His gun database was nowhere near complete. At the end of 1922, Waite headed to Europe to gather the same information about European guns that he had collected about American firearms. He spoke only English and he became ill frequently on his travels, but he found helpful people wherever he went. Concerned that his age would prevent him from finishing his work, Waite rushed to complete his quest. At the end of a year, his job was done. Waite had collected a huge amount of information on firearms, which he carefully catalogued, as well as 1,500 sample guns.

Once again, Waite did not have time to relax with his findings. Shortly after he returned to the United States, a sheriff showed Waite a bullet and asked him to identify what kind of gun had fired it. Waite's opinion was that it had come from a certain kind of Belgian revolver. One of the sheriff's suspects was a Belgian man, who confessed when confronted with this information. While the case ended neatly enough, Waite realized that there needed to be a way to identify markings on bullets as coming from a particular gun, not just a type of gun. The question was: How could bullet markings be systematically examined?

Waite had a microscope made that had bullet holders and special measurement scales, but he felt he was too old to learn to use it. His eyesight wasn't strong enough and his hands weren't steady. It was time to build a forensic ballistics team. Charles Waite was joined by physicist John Fisher and chemist and photographer Philip Gravelle. Together, in 1923, they began the world's first Bureau of Forensic Ballistics in New York.

Fisher had previously helped to develop a medical instrument called the cystoscope, which sent thin tubes with tiny lamps into the bladder and kidneys in order to view them. He thought that a version of this device would help Waite inspect the insides of guns, so he made a helixometer—a long, hollow probe with a lamp and magnifier on one end.

In order to test the theory that each gun created unique markings on bullets, Gravelle took thousands of photographs of bullets fired into cotton (to protect them from damage) and compared them. He concluded that the unique marking theory was true, but felt that he had to do more research to prove it. In order to take the weak link—the human memory—out of his attempts to compare two bullets under a microscope, Gravelle invented a microscope that enabled him to look at two bullets at the same time. He no longer had to remember what the first bullet looked like while examining the second—with the bullets side by side, the similarities and differences showed clearly. The comparison microscope proved to be a vital tool for firearms specialists.

The third person to join Waite was a 34-year-old doctor named Calvin Goddard. Goddard was from Baltimore and had attended Johns Hopkins University, graduating in 1915. He spent 1916-1920 in Europe with the United States Army in the Medical Corps. Before returning to the United States, Goddard switched from the Medical Corps to Ordnance—the section in charge of weapons and ammunition.

Although Goddard's education was in medicine, he had become fascinated with guns as a young boy, and he actually made his own revolvers. He held two medical teaching positions upon his return from the war, but, in 1924, Goddard decided to learn more about firearms identification. He asked Albert Hamilton (the Stielow case "expert," who was still well known in the field) about becoming a ballistics specialist. He found Hamilton to be less than impressive and continued his medical career.

In 1925, however, Goddard met Waite and jumped on board at the Bureau of Forensic Ballistics. Goddard was soon using Gravelle's comparison microscope with great skill, identifying differences even between bullets shot by the same type of gun and made with the same tools. The markings on bullets were completely individual, Goddard found, and he set about convincing courts of that.

But Goddard's path was not entirely easy. Gravelle and Fisher left the Bureau after a short time—due to lack of business—and Waite died of a heart attack on November 14, 1926. Charles Waite had been right that he had not had much time left, but he had found someone who felt as passionately about using ballistics for justice as he did. Goddard became the director of the Bureau and kept working.

In June 1927, Goddard approached the defense and prosecution teams of the famous Sacco and Vanzetti case and offered his services. Nicola Sacco and Bartolomeo Vanzetti, two Italian anarchists, had been found guilty of murdering the paymaster and a guard at a shoe factory in South Braintree, Massachusetts, and stealing the $16,000 payroll. The crime occurred in April 1920 and the two were found guilty in 1921, but their appeals had delayed their executions for six years. Many people around the world thought Sacco and Vanzetti had been convicted because of their political beliefs, not for the crimes for which they had been accused. Had they really committed the murders?

Their defense lawyers were not interested in Goddard's opinion. They already had opinions that they liked—one of which was from Albert Hamilton. In 1923, he said nothing found at the scene of the crime—neither the bullets in the bodies nor the cartridges—could have come from Sacco's or Vanzetti's

**anarchist:** a person who believes that all forms of government are oppressive and should be abolished

*Bartolomeo Vanzetti (center) and Nicola Sacco (right), manacled together, await their trial.*

gun. During his testimony, Hamilton took apart Sacco's Colt pistol as well as two new Colt pistols to illustrate his points. Then, when he put them back together, he put the new ones in his pockets to take home. The judge was suspicious and ordered him to leave the new guns. It was discovered that Sacco's gun had a new barrel and the old barrel was on one of the new guns. Hamilton claimed that someone on the prosecution side had done the switch, but the goal of his testimony—to win the defendants a new trial—was unsuccessful.

The prosecution, however, accepted Goddard's offer to examine the evidence with his comparison microscope. One of the other experts for the defense, Augustus Gill, agreed to be present. Gill thought the microscope so impressive that he said he would accept Goddard's conclusion, even if it went against his own findings. Goddard determined that a bullet used in the murder had come from Sacco's gun and no other. Gill looked through the microscope himself and said, "Well, what do you know about that?" He and another of the defense experts withdrew from the defense's team. Based on this evidence, the Massachusetts governor did not pardon Sacco and Vanzetti, and they were executed on August 23, 1927.

Goddard's next big break came in 1929, when he was called to Chicago by the grand jury investigating the St. Valentine's Day Massacre. Gangster Al Capone had wanted to eliminate Bugs Moran, his competitor in the illegal liquor trade, and had devised a plan to kill Moran and his associates. Moran's people were inside a parking garage waiting for Moran when a car full of men in police uniforms drove up. It seemed like a raid—until the "cops" started shooting. Seven people were killed.

Capone was in Florida during the massacre and said he didn't have anything to do with it. Police corruption in Chicago was so common at the time that newspapers printed stories saying real police officers had done the killings. Goddard ran tests on all of the guns in the police department to determine if any had been involved. He found no matches

In 1961, Jac Weller and Frank Jury, two American forensic ballistics experts, held new tests comparing Sacco's pistol and the murder bullets and shells. They concluded that Goddard had been correct.

In 1919, the United States established laws making the manufacture and sale of alcoholic beverages illegal. During this period, called Prohibition, many people broke the laws—and often made a lot of money doing so. The laws banning alcohol were repealed in 1933.

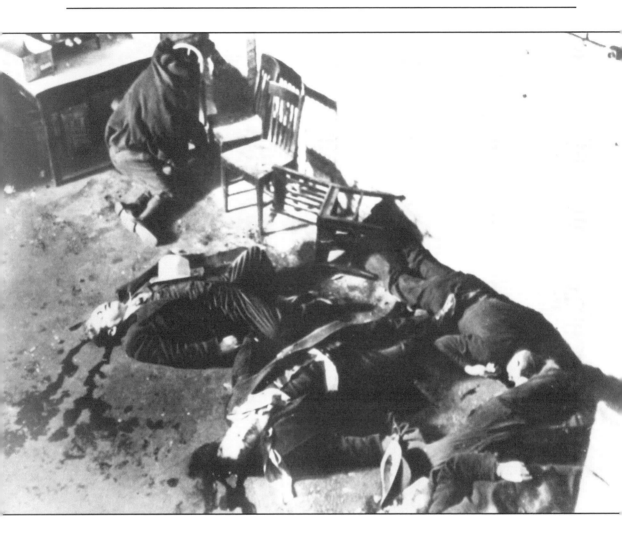

*The grisly scene in a Chicago garage following the St. Valentine's Day Massacre*

between the police weapons and the murder bullets, which he concluded were from two different .45-caliber Thompson machine guns.

The big break in the case came ten months later, in December 1929. Police found a hoard of weapons, including two Thompson machine guns, when they were searching the apartment of a suspect accused of shooting a police officer. Goddard shot test bullets from the machine guns into containers of cotton. Then he spent hours comparing them to the bullets used in the St. Valentine's Day Massacre.

He concluded they were a match. The suspect, Fred Burke, was a professional killer who had previously worked for Capone. The pieces had fallen into place. Burke was sentenced to life imprisonment for his more recent crimes, however, and was never tried for the Massacre. The other two men suspected of being involved in the killings were found shot to death, apparently by Bugs Moran.

*The man behind the St. Valentine's Day Massacre, as well as many other crimes, Al Capone (1899-1947) was imprisoned for income tax evasion in 1931.*

## THE RESULT

Goddard's painstaking work on the St. Valentine's Day Massacre impressed prominent Chicago residents. They decided to ask Goddard to found and direct a new forensic laboratory in Illinois. He agreed to give up his New York lab and start the Scientific Crime Detection Laboratory on the campus of Northwestern University in Evanston. Goddard was also named a professor of political science at the university. Before opening the lab in 1930, Goddard spent three months in Europe, visiting forensic centers in 13 countries. His laboratory would be the first comprehensive crime center in the United States.

Although the lab was a great resource, handling hundreds of firearms cases a year, the work was not smooth sailing for Goddard. He carried a gun wherever he went for years because he thought Al Capone might seek revenge. An armed guard stood outside his door and checked in the room whenever a shot was fired—which must have been fairly often, considering all of Goddard's tests!

But the toughest problem facing Goddard was money. In 1934, during the Great Depression, he worked without pay for the entire year and then had to resign. The ballistics center that Charles Waite had envisioned—one that would be a resource for the whole country—became a reality in the form of the ballistics department at the Federal Bureau of Investigation (FBI), which Goddard helped to set up. In the following years, Goddard was awarded

fellowships by the Guggenheim Foundation and the Oberlander Trust, which gave him the chance to continue his work. In 1941, at age 50, Goddard returned to active service in the army. He became a historian for the Ordnance Department, a field he continued to work in until the year before his death in 1955.

*A section of Goddard's gun collection, housed at the Scientific Crime Detection Laboratory at Northwestern University*

Firearm identification has become a vital, well-established part of forensics. The field has changed over the years as scientists have learned more about ballistics. For instance, shooting guns into cotton to create test bullets for comparison with suspect bullets was common practice—until someone realized that the cotton fibers affected what scientists could learn from the bullets. Now test bullets are commonly shot into water tanks.

In another example of how the field of ballistics has changed, British police officers in 1933 were instructed to lift suspect weapons by sticking a metal rod down the gun barrel rather than grabbing them with their hands. Contemporary police officers, however, are told not to put anything down the barrel because instruments such as modern helixometers can spot tiny details on the inside of a gun. Metal rods or other objects can mar these details.

Examining gunshot residue has become an important source of information in the field of ballistics. Ammunition consists of two basic parts, the bullet and the powder that propels the bullet. When the trigger is pulled on a gun, the powder ignites and forms gases that expand so quickly they propel the bullet from the gun. But not all of this powder burns. Some of the powder can remain on the hand of the person who fired the weapon. Residue can help experts determine if a proposed scenario of events at a crime scene could have occurred. For instance, gunshot residue on a shooting victim can indicate how close the person was to the gun when it was fired. Experts can also compare the pattern, size, and concentration of residue at a crime scene with the residue from a test firing of a suspect gun.

One thing that has not changed over the years, though, is the fact that bullets can "talk" about the gun that fired them. Ballistics pioneers Charles Waite and Calvin Goddard journeyed a great distance, both literally and metaphorically, to enable others to "hear" them.

*Another advance used in ballistics is the electron microscope, an instrument that can find markings on bullets not visible with a regular microscope. Here weapons expert Robert Hathaway holds a .45-caliber handgun with its fired ammunition shown magnified.*

# CHAPTER FIVE

# Mildred Trotter
# and Forensic Anthropology

Older crimes are the most difficult to solve. Evidence fades, and witnesses may be unreachable, but even in such cases, there are ways to search out the facts. And one of the most important ways is to find information from the bones of the victim.

What can we discover from bones? Early physical anthropologists studied bones to uncover information about the evolution of human beings and the origins of the races. Forensic anthropologists analyze bones to help solve other kinds of mysteries. When remains are found, forensic anthropologists working on the case begin by determining if the bones are human. If so, they must then discern the age of the bones and whether they belonged to more than one person.

To find answers to these and other questions, forensic anthropologists must have a profound knowledge of human anatomy. They also need details about the location where the remains were

*Prominent physical anthropologist and honored anatomy professor Mildred Trotter (1899-1991) earned the title "bone detective" for her contributions to forensic science.*

**anthropology:** a scientific study of the origin, behavior, and the physical, social, and cultural development of human beings

**decompose:** to break down into components; to decay or cause to rot

*George Parkman (1790-1849)*

**cadaver:** a dead body, especially one intended for dissection

discovered—for example, whether any artifacts were located with them, how deep the body was buried, and in what type of soil. When decomposed remains are found, law enforcement personnel hope that they can learn the race, sex, age, height, and possibly even more from forensic anthropologists.

In 1849, the disappearance of Dr. George Parkman spurred forensic anthropology's first known case. One evening, Parkman went to Dr. John White Webster's laboratory at Harvard Medical School to collect payment of a debt and was never seen again. Webster claimed that he had paid Parkman, who then left. Webster had both motive and opportunity to murder Parkman, but a police search of his laboratory and office did not turn up any evidence of wrongdoing.

The breakthrough in the case came when Ephraim Littlefield, the medical school janitor, did a little investigating on his own. He found part of a torso and two pieces of leg, both still covered with flesh, in the vault where cadavers used in anatomy classes were kept. The discovery prompted the police to do another, more careful search of Webster's office. This time, they discovered bones in a tea chest and a set of charred false teeth in the furnace. Were the bones from a medical-school cadaver, cut off and hidden by prankster students? Were they from one body or several?

The police brought in some experts—Harvard Medical School dean Oliver Wendell Holmes, anatomist Jeffries Wyman, and Nathan Cooley Keep, Parkman's dentist—to help solve the case. Holmes and Wyman determined that the bones came from one body. As there were no signs that the body had been embalmed—treated with preservatives to prevent decay—they knew that it couldn't be a cadaver belonging to the medical school. The anatomists then estimated that the height and age of the body matched Parkman. Wyman noted that the section of chest the janitor had found was extremely hairy, and that Parkman had been an unusually hairy man.

The next testimony—that of Parkman's dentist—also packed a punch. Keep said that four years ago he had made dentures for George Parkman using a distinctive cast. He had then filed them down when Parkman complained there was no room for his tongue. Not only did the teeth found in Webster's office match Keep's cast, but Keep's file marks were visible as well. Faced with the evidence, John Webster admitted that he had killed George Parkman in a fit of anger and dismembered the body. Webster was convicted, and he was hanged on August 30, 1850.

To honor Parkman, Harvard established a professorship of anatomy in his name. One holder of this professorship, Thomas Dwight, made a contribution to the development of forensic anthropology when he became the first American to publish a paper on skeletal differences in 1878. At that time, conducting scholarly research on spotting the variance among skeletons and using those differences to identify a skeleton was a new concept.

Then, on February 3, 1899, a girl was born whose contributions to forensic anthropology would

*John Webster (1793-1850)*

*Jeffries Wyman (1814-1874)*

*Oliver Wendell Holmes (1809-1894)*

be long lasting. Mildred Trotter, daughter of James and Jennie B. Trotter, grew up on a farm in Monaca, Pennsylvania. She attended Beaver High School, where the principal informed her family that she should take home economics instead of geometry. His reason? Home economics would be more "appropriate" for a girl. Mildred took geometry.

After graduating from high school in 1916, Mildred went to Mount Holyoke College in Massachusetts. When she took zoology her sophomore year, she became hooked on science. She followed up with classes in comparative anatomy, embryology, and bacteriology, as well as additional zoology coursework. Mildred found the zoology department head, Dr. Ann Haven Morgan, and two of the other professors, Dr. Christianna Smith and Dr. Elizabeth Adams, inspiring. For her entire career, Mildred would keep photographs of the three professors in her office. Her dedication to Mount Holyoke would never waver because, as she would explain later, "It made me."

After earning her degree in 1920, Mildred Trotter had two job offers from which to choose. One was as a high school biology teacher in her home state for $1,650 a year. The other was as a researcher for Washington University School of Medicine in St. Louis, Missouri, with an annual salary of $1,000. Professor Smith had recommended her to Dr. C. H. Danforth, an associate professor of anatomy at Washington who was looking for a bright college graduate to work with him. Once Trotter learned that she would earn credit toward a master's

*Mildred Trotter's senior photograph from Mount Holyoke College*

*Two of Mildred Trotter's professors and mentors at Mount Holyoke College, Christianna Smith (left) and Ann Haven Morgan, photographed at around the time that Trotter graduated in 1920*

degree in anatomy with her work at Washington, her mind was made up. Even though the pay was less, Trotter said she really "wanted to be where the science was."

At the university, the chair of the anatomy department, Dr. Robert J. Terry (1871-1966), influenced Trotter's work, and later her teaching style. He recommended studying from life rather than studying books. The professor and his assistant

When Mildred Trotter began her career at Washington University, she studied facial hair and discovered that men and women have about the same number of facial hair follicles (the depression in the skin from which hair emerges), but women's are less developed. During her study, Trotter marked each follicle on a section of her leg with a drop of India ink. Since the marks would be permanent (similar to a tattoo), Trotter put the drops "where I thought it would never show." To her chagrin, though, skirt lengths changed.

collected skeletons from dissected cadavers and Trotter learned to clean the bones of tissue, a process called maceration. She agreed with Terry's philosophy and said, "It's important for students to know that textbooks may not describe their cadaver. Learning to observe is one of the chief benefits of studying anatomy."

By 1922, Trotter's studies were turning into published papers. She earned her master's degree and her Ph.D. in anatomy by 1924 and was made an instructor in the department. Trotter was awarded a National Research Council Fellowship and studied physical anthropology at Oxford University in England from 1925 to 1926.

Her commitment to science left no room for nervousness—to Trotter, a cadaver was an object to be studied, not something to fear. "When you work with dead people you don't become calloused, but it becomes an interesting job," she said. "The attitude of our culture toward death is silly. We all know we have to die."

In 1930, the university promoted Trotter to an associate professor of anatomy, but discrimination against women in the academic world slowed her progress. She remained in that position for 16 years. Despite being advised not to, Trotter finally went in 1946 to the department head, Dr. E. V. Cowdry, and asked him, "In what way am I deficient for promotion?" He determined that she was proficient in every way, and, at last, Mildred Trotter received her full professorship.

## THE BREAKTHROUGH

World War II increased Trotter's workload. Classes were taught more intensively in an effort to speed up the education of doctors much needed by the military. In addition to teaching, Trotter acted as a consultant for the U.S. Public Health Service on the anatomical aspects of anesthesia. After the war was over, she learned that the U.S. Army was in need of an anthropologist to identify the remains of war dead from the Pacific front, and she applied. The army had set up a Central Identification Laboratory in Hawaii in 1947. Trotter took a leave of absence from Washington University and spent 14 months in Hawaii. Once she was at her post, Trotter discovered that her age and sex had been a concern for the army and had caused a delay to her acceptance.

*Mildred Trotter, photographed not long before she left for Hawaii. In this study at Washington University, she measured sections of the lower spine and pelvis to help doctors inject spinal anesthetics more accurately.*

As always, Trotter made the most of her opportunity, though her task was not an easy one. The army had records of missing soldiers and where they had been fighting. From these files, she had to identify the remains by comparing skeletons to old X-rays, dental charts, army measurements of recruits, and descriptions provided by relatives. Identified remains were returned to the United States for reburial.

Determining the age of a body at the time of its death is possible because, as Trotter observed, "the human skeleton operates on a time table." For instance, infants are born with an opening on the top of their skulls that gradually closes by the toddler years. Also, upper-arm bones don't become completely ossified—when cartilage and other soft tissues have hardened into bone—until a person reaches age 20. Collarbones ossify when a person is between the ages of 25 and 28.

Another important clue to a skeleton's age, Trotter said, is the teeth. "They usually are worn down in an older person. But in order to be accurate, you must know the person's culture," she noted. This will tell you the types of food—hard, soft, tough—that person would most often have eaten.

In her efforts to identify remains, Trotter would study even the smallest details. Sounding a bit like the fictional detective Sherlock Holmes, she said, "Sometimes you can ascertain by the joint surfaces what a person's occupation was." A worn shoulder bone, for instance, might indicate the person had carried heavy loads.

But while working to identify the dead soldiers, Trotter realized that the accepted method of estimating a skeleton's height—derived from a nineteenth-century French study—was not sufficiently accurate when applied to modern Americans. Using this method, the height estimates she made were off by as much as 1.7 inches. Trotter dedicated herself to finding another equation that would more accurately predict height.

*Mildred Trotter examining a human bone*

First, Trotter persuaded the commander of the U.S. Army in the Pacific to allow her to measure bones of the war dead who had been identified. By measuring skeletons for which heights were already known, she planned to create a calculation that would enable scientists to take a single bone and accurately estimate how tall that person had been when alive.

The army was slow to allow her to measure bodies that had already been identified. But after six months of explaining that the current method for estimating height seemed outdated, Trotter received permission. She and her staff spent months measuring 790 male skeletons (710 white; 80 African American).

Trotter's hard work paid off. She found an equation using the length of the femur, also known as the thigh bone, that accurately predicted how tall a person had been. To calculate the height, a researcher multiplied the length of the femur by 2.38. That sum plus 24.1771 inches equaled a person's height.

While Trotter was in Hawaii, her reputation for skeletal identification reached the ears of the Hawaiian police, who came to her with a skeleton found in a ravine. They had no idea who it was, but hoped she could point them in the right direction. Once she studied it and gave them her conclusions, the police told her, "You have given us everything about him but his name."

## THE RESULT

After her return from Hawaii, Trotter continued teaching at Washington University, with another, briefer trip in 1951 to the Philippine Islands to identify war dead. Trotter's equation for estimating height was so well researched and accurate that over 50 years later it continues to be used by forensic specialists, including the FBI.

Trotter's research projects, which number over a hundred, have been used by physical anthropologists, historians, nutritionists, and even the National Aeronautics and Space Administration (NASA). "She has been responsible for the largest single increase in our knowledge of bones," said her colleague, Dr. Stanley Garn, a nutrition professor. "In addition, by providing hard data on skeletal weights and therefore adult bone loss, Trotter stimulated hundreds of investigations." Among Trotter's other findings, she observed that once a person has reached full growth, his or her height decreases approximately half an inch per 20 years ever after.

While Mildred Trotter taught at Washington University, she also helped St. Louis police officers identify remains, including one instance when she proved that bones the police thought belonged to an animal were actually those of an infant.

Although she retired in 1967, she continued working, publishing a dozen research papers after her retirement. In 1985, Trotter, known as "Trot" to her colleagues and students, had a stroke while visiting South Africa. She died on August 23, 1991, at

*Trotter taught two Nobel Prize-winning scientists, Daniel Nathans and Earl Sutherland, pictured here. Sutherland received his prize in 1971 for his research on how hormones work.*

the age of 92. Her love of research and eye for spotting the subtle distinctions between skeletons made her one of the world's great "bone detectives." As Trot said herself, "Each human body is different; the ability to discern the differences is a crucial part of medicine."

That ability to discern differences is needed in many cases when there would be no other hope of identification otherwise. In 1978, John Wayne Gacy Jr. confessed that he had murdered 33 young men and buried many in a crawl space under his home. Gacy refused to identify the people that he had killed; therefore, the ones that could not be named based on their dental records had to be examined by skilled forensic anthropologists. Families whose children were missing sent physical descriptions of them to the police and anxiously awaited word. All but 9 of the victims were identified.

Another modern technique that forensic anthropologists use to identify the dead is facial reconstruction. First, scientists glue tissue depth markers on the person's skull (or on a plaster case of the skull). Marker lengths depend on the person's age, sex, and race, all factors that can be determined from studying the skull and other bones. Glass eyes are then added, then layers of clay. Based on the size and shape of the skull, the face reconstructionist sculpts a nose, mouth, and other facial features.

Facial reconstructions are made when a body cannot be identified based on dental records, matching missing persons reports, or other conventional methods.

*Serial killer John Wayne Gacy Jr. was executed by lethal injection in Illinois on May 10, 1994.*

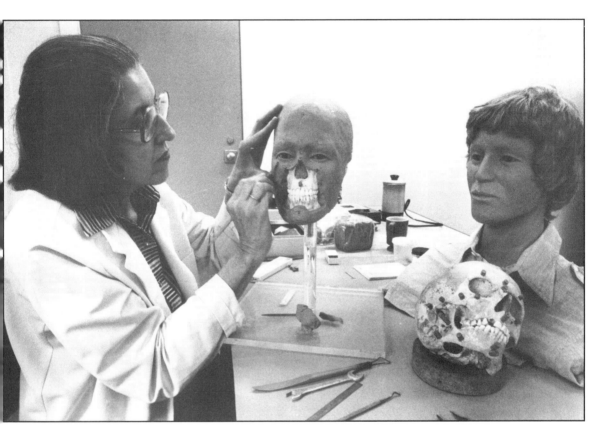

Facial reconstruction was also used to help identify some of Gacy's murder victims. Betty Pat Gatliff adds modeling clay to the skull of one of the victims. Pegs mark the depth of soft tissue on a skull (lower right). Clay is then applied over these markers and carefully modeled to create features. Photographs of the completed reconstructions, like the one behind the skull, were released to the press in the hope that someone would recognize the young men.

# CHAPTER SIX

# Jacques Penry
# and Photo-FIT

How can the police help witnesses to a crime provide an identification of a suspect? The most basic way is to write down a verbal description given by the witness. The description they would pass along to other officers and the public might look something like this: Caucasian male, brown hair, brown eyes, 25 to 30 years old, six feet tall, wearing a blue T-shirt and jeans, sneakers. Any piercings, tattoos, warts, birthmarks, or other distinctive markings would be noted. This information is a good starting point, but if the witness has a detailed memory of the perpetrator's face, law enforcement agencies want to use that information, too.

One way of having witnesses identify a suspect is to have them look at "mug shot" albums, which are books containing full-face and profile photos of previously arrested individuals. If suspects have no prior arrests, however, witnesses won't find them in the books. Also, if witnesses have to look through

*In 1970, Jacques Penry demonstrated his innovative Photo-FIT system by assembling a likeness of James Callaghan (in his hand), the soon-to-be prime minister of Britain.*

*A police detective searching through a mug shot album*

thousands of photos before finding the culprit, the face they remember may start to blur and they may feel unsure about the photo they choose.

Another facial identification method is the police artist sketch. With this approach, a witness describes the suspect's face to a police artist, who produces a drawing. The result can be changed on the basis of the witness's responses until it matches his or her memory of the suspect's face. The sketches can be realistic and useful, but the limitations to this approach include the cost of hiring a police sketch artist and the amount of time it takes to create a successful sketch.

In 1959, American law enforcement officials came up with a method that allowed any police officer to be an artist. Called Identi-Kit, this system was made up of a set of transparencies—see-through sheets of plastic—printed with drawings of individual features such as noses, eyes, and chins. The transparencies could be layered to create a whole face. A special pencil was included to allow the users to customize the combined picture, known as a composite.

Identi-Kit pleased police officers because they could use the system without much training, unlike methods requiring a sketch artist. Since witnesses could look at the transparencies, it enabled them to recognize features by sight rather than depending solely on their ability to describe a suspect. One drawback of the system, however, was that it was two-dimensional. Was it possible for police officers to add more realism to their facial composites of suspects?

A Canadian living in England named Jacques Penry had been studying "facial topography" since the early years of the twentieth century. In 1938, while preparing his first book, *Character from the Face*, Penry had the idea of "building a face" from photographs. He discovered that it was possible to take features from one face and combine them with features from another face. Penry found that this

**topography:** the surface features of a place or region

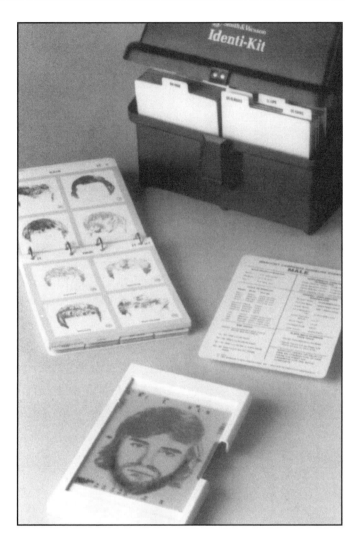

*The Identi-Kit built a face feature by feature, beginning with the outline of the lower face and then adding eyes, nose, lips, and hair all based on the estimated age of the suspect.*

worked only when the photographs were taken at the same angle and enlarged to the same size. He also realized that the photographs had to be cropped at particular facial points for this process to be realistic. The basic plan for making a facial composite system was percolating in Penry's brain, but he didn't have access to enough photographs to build a comprehensive collection of facial features. His focus also was not on police work.

Penry studied faces because he believed that there was a link between a person's physique and his or her personality. In 1952, Penry's second book, *The Face of Man*, was published. This book explained his classification system for faces. While developing his system, he sketched enough facial features to make 50 million composite faces—enough to create the facial composite system. He did not act on his idea until 1968, however, when he approached the British Home Office Police and offered to make a facial identification system. The Home Office contracted with Penry to produce a kit of Caucasian male photographic facial segments, full-view and profile.

## THE BREAKTHROUGH

The British police permitted Penry to use photographs in their archives to create his kit. To ensure anonymity of the people in the photographs, he "borrowed" a nose here, a pair of eyes there, and made sure that no entire face was used. "Without access to such archives," Penry said, "it would have been virtually impossible to make a really efficient and comprehensive facial identification system." The system was initially called PFIT for Penry Facial Identification Technique, but the press dubbed it "Photo-FIT."

Penry worked hard to select as many variations as possible for his collection of features. Having researched faces for over 30 years, Penry felt confident that his knowledge would enable him to provide a thorough assortment of choices. He picked more than 500 features and divided them into five groups: forehead/hairline, eyes, nose, mouth, and lower frame contour, including the chin. From those 500 features, 5 billion individual faces could be assembled.

Penry had to make sure that all the features would fit together smoothly and create a realistic-looking face. All of the photographs had to be enlarged to achieve this. The photographs he used had been taken by many different people and in many different situations over the years. The focus, lighting, and distance varied from subject to subject. So, Penry explained, he also had to "determine and establish the norm of tone, light, and contrast to which the whole should conform." Finally, he added a selection of what he called "accessories"—hats, glasses, mustaches, beards, and age lines—which made the number of possible appearances even greater.

After overcoming these problems, Penry still had to grapple with the actual construction of the Photo-FIT kit itself. He glued the photographs onto thin pieces of cardboard and then cut them to size. "I did not realize that in dry or centrally-heated conditions the parts would curl and give much difficulty and frustration to those who later tested the prototype," he said. In addition, Penry created an index of the kit's 500 original features, which he numbered, coded, and labeled with a description.

As a complement to Photo-FIT, Penry wrote a book called *Looking at Faces and Remembering Them: A Guide to Facial Identification*. This book was intended to help potential witnesses learn how to classify faces for easy identification. "We are all potential witnesses," said Penry, but he noted the ability to identify a face was especially important for people working in professions such as security or banking. It would be useful for them to be able to recognize many people or to accurately describe someone suspected of a crime.

Witnesses are often distracted by the expression on a culprit's face, Penry explained, and often describe the emotions of the culprit better than the features. "It is the *mobility* of the facial pattern which so often leads us astray, the constant interplay of facial muscles in response to thought and emotion," he said. Also, items such as glasses or facial hair

The face has about 150 muscles.

tend to be remembered more clearly than the shape of a nose. Accessories can change the look of a face, as well. For instance, a wide-brimmed hat may make a face appear shorter than it is.

Making facial identification as reliable as possible makes justice possible, said Penry. He wanted witnesses to see faces as "classifiable structures" made up of physical shapes, rather than as conveyors of emotion. Penry encouraged witnesses to sketch their own profile outlines of suspects' faces and write down notes while the memory was still fresh.

Penry's kit was tested by the police in Bristol and Birmingham and by New Scotland Yard. During that time, John Waddington, Ltd., a company in Leeds, England, began manufacture of Photo-FIT. Penry thought this was a courageous move because "at that time they could not be given assurance of a single order from the Home Office or elsewhere." When Photo-FIT did receive approval by the police, the company had the kit ready to sell.

## THE RESULT

In 1970, the full-view Caucasian male kit was released. Penry then produced an Afro-Asian supplement, which made possible the creation of 500 million separate faces. After this, he created the profile Caucasian male kit. Penry did not want the police to focus exclusively on full-view face identification; he thought that this approach risked losing

*A law officer works with a witness to reconstruct the face of a suspect using Photo-FIT features.*

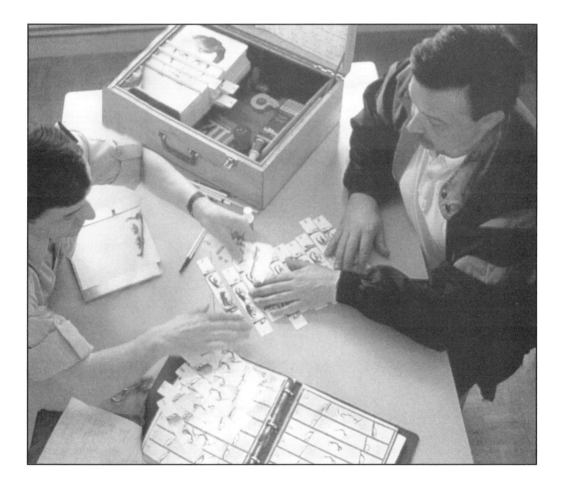

valuable information from witnesses who only saw a side view of a suspect. His profile kit matched the front-view kit exactly, meaning that profile nose number 33 is from the same person as front-view nose 33.

Three years later, after receiving help from the Royal Canadian Mounted Police, Penry issued a North American Indian supplement. In the meantime, Penry had also decided to add annual updates. He saw the need to keep up with modern hairstyles, hats, glasses, and other accessories that changed fairly rapidly. In 1973, the Caucasian kit had 204 foreheads/hairstyles, 96 pairs of eyes, 89 noses, 101 mouths, and 74 cheek/chin sections, forming some 15 billion possible combinations. By 1974, Penry had developed a female supplement, which had many features interchangeable with the male kit. He also custom-designed features and accessories for international law enforcement agencies.

As of 1974, Photo-FIT was being used everywhere from Argentina to Iceland, Peru to Nigeria. In the mid-1970s, the Home Office in England added "cognitive interview" techniques to the Photo-FIT training courses. These techniques were added to help the police officers draw out accurate information from witnesses.

In the mid-1970s, Photo-FIT ran into some copyright problems in the United States and no more updates were issued for Photo-FIT there. Consequently, the accessories began to become outdated. Police departments around the world, however, continued to use the Photo-FIT kit.

While the Photo-FIT kit itself was growing outdated, the concept of Photo-FIT was being adapted to a new tool becoming available to the police—computers. Having the facial composite on the computer allowed for many exciting possibilities. With forensic facial identification programs, the computer user can manipulate the features on the face any number of ways—making the ears asymmetrical, flattening the nose, lengthening the mouth, and so on. Like the original Photo-FIT, these computer programs allow any police officer to create a facial composite regardless of his or her lack of artistic talent.

There is, however, still a role for traditional police sketch artists to play. Highly skilled sketch artists can often obtain detailed information from witnesses and produce impressive drawings. Some of the most famous recent sketches were of Theodore Kaczynski, known as the Unabomber. He killed 3 people and injured 25 in 16 different bombing attacks from 1978 through 1995. Protesting what he viewed as the evils of technology, Kaczynski mailed letter and package bombs, usually to people connected with advances in technology, and set traps in public places. In 1987 in Salt Lake City, he disguised a bomb as a piece of wood with nails sticking out. A shop owner detonated the bomb while trying to move the obstacle and was severely injured.

Moments before the explosion, a woman had glimpsed Kaczynski's face. Several police artists created sketches from her description. One by artist Jeanne Boylan became very well known and widely

*This sketch by an FBI artist was the first of several made of the Unabomber.*

*Theodore Kaczynski being escorted by U.S. marshals from the federal courthouse in Helena, Montana, in 1996. He was tried the following year; in January 1998 he pleaded guilty under an agreement that spared him from the death penalty.*

circulated. These sketches were the only likeness police and FBI agents had during the 17 years they searched for Kaczynski. When he was arrested in April 1996 at his remote Montana cabin, some FBI agents wore T-shirts bearing Boylan's portrait.

But even police sketch artists can be helped by computers. The Hong Kong Police Force has only three artists who handle as many as 20 cases a day. They don't have time to spend hours on a drawing, so they use computer software to make final adjustments to their original sketches.

Another new computerized tool is the ability to compare a facial composite with a mug shot database. For example, during a September 1997 carjacking in California, the victim was able to see the culprit well enough for a composite to be created. A computer program came up with a selection of mug shots similar to the composite, and the police created a photo lineup for the victim to view. Both the victim and another witness chose the same suspect, who was later arrested.

Imaging specialists are working on adding a third dimension to photograph composites. BSB Forensic, a London-based company, has a goal of building a national database of 3-D photographs using a three-dimensional camera system developed by high-tech specialists. With 3-D, witnesses can move the angle around to replicate the way they saw the suspect most clearly. BSB Forensic also wants police departments to have the capability to create 3-D photos from video footage. If this plan becomes operational, witness composites could be compared with mug shots in three dimensions.

British forensic specialists have also suggested that sometime in the next 10 years, they might have the capability to create composite images based on data derived from bits of a person's DNA left behind at a crime scene.

Although many police forces now use computer technology rather than Penry's old Photo-FIT kit, his idea was influential enough that electronic composites are often still referred to as "photofits."

# CHAPTER SEVEN

# Alec Jeffreys and DNA Fingerprints

In the beginning of the twentieth century, Austrian physician Karl Landsteiner told the world about an exciting new discovery. Folklore had always maintained that each person's blood was different. Early attempts at blood transfusions seemed to confirm this wisdom; the procedure was as likely to kill as to cure the patient.

Landsteiner found that there were actually four distinct types of human blood, differentiated by antigens in the blood. (Antigens cause the body to produce antibodies, which fight disease and infection.) Landsteiner classified blood as type A if it contained a substance called antigen A; B if it contained antigen B; AB if it contained both; and O if it contained neither. When blood with one antigen is given to someone who does not have that antigen, the red blood cells clump together, which can cause death. Landsteiner's breakthrough earned him a Nobel Prize in 1930.

*Professor Sir Alec Jeffreys (b. 1950), with a DNA fingerprint produced by a technique he invented. These "prints," which resemble a pattern of bands or stripes on X-ray film, have dramatically changed forensic science.*

*Karl Landsteiner (1868-1943) moved to the United States in 1922, where he joined the staff of the Rockefeller Institute for Medical Research (now Rockefeller University).*

The commonest type of blood is O; 45 percent of the U.S. population has this blood type, 42 percent has A, and 10 percent B. Only 3 percent of Americans have type AB.

In 1915, Italian professor Leone Lattes developed the first test for identifying the blood type of dried stains.

Landsteiner's work was useful in forensics as well as in medicine. For instance, if a murder or assault suspect said that he bled on his shirt after he cut himself shaving, the blood could be analyzed to confirm whether or not it was his blood type—or that of the victim. Blood-typing became an accepted tool in criminal investigations.

Although the discovery of blood types was a tremendous step in the science of identifying people, it was a return to the idea that each person's blood is unique that allowed the next step. It's not the blood itself, of course, that is individual, but rather the molecular makeup of the cells found in blood—and other parts of the body.

The scientist who made this leap was born in Oxford, England, on January 9, 1950. His name was Alec Jeffreys. When he was eight years old, his father gave him a chemistry set and microscope. From then on, science fascinated Alec. When he went to Oxford University in 1968, he studied biochemistry, the combination of biology and chemistry. The aspect of biochemistry that interested Jeffreys most was genetics—the study of how traits, such as eye color, are passed on from parents to their offspring. To learn more about it, Jeffreys went on to earn a Ph.D. in human genetics at Oxford. In 1975, he traveled to Amsterdam, The Netherlands, to work with Dr. Richard Flavell. Their goal was to see if they could detect individual genes, the basic unit of inheritance that determines a particular characteristic in an organism, in human DNA.

DNA, short for deoxyribonucleic acid, is found in almost every living cell in animals, plants, bacteria, and other microorganisms. DNA carries the genetic information in the cell and consists of two long chains of chemical compounds called nucleotides twisted into the shape of a spiral known as a double helix. These twin spirals are joined by four interlocking chemical bases—adenine paired with thymine and cytosine paired with guanine. Genes are found along chromosomes in sequences of these chemical bases. All of the information for each individual's genetic makeup is packed into each cell.

**cell:** the smallest unit of living things. The cell is made up of a substance called protoplasm and surrounded by a thin membrane. Most cells have a central part called a nucleus surrounded by a clear fluid called cytoplasm. In many-celled animals and plants, such as humans and trees, different types of cells have specific functions.

**chromosome:** the tiny, thread-like parts of a cell that develop just before a cell divides and carry the genes of heredity

**enzyme:** a complex substance found in living things that controls a chemical reaction without being changed itself. An average cell in the human body contains about 3,000 different enzymes.

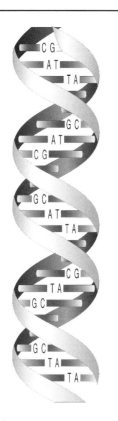

*The letters A, T, G, and C represent the four nitrogen bases in the structure of DNA. Adenine always combines with thymine and cytosine always bonds with guanine.*

In their research on DNA in Amsterdam, Jeffreys and Flavell used a technique developed by Edwin Southern in 1975. This technique involves using enzymes that recognize combinations of base patterns. The enzymes cause a chemical reaction that can snip apart DNA at specific points, like a pair of scissors, leaving fragments of various sizes.

These fragments of the DNA are separated from each other using an electric field. Then probes—short, single-stranded portions of synthetic DNA with radioactive atoms—are added. The probes target specific bases of the sample and automatically pair with them. X-rays can be made of these DNA segments; dark bands develop at the probe sites.

Jeffreys left Amsterdam in the late 1970s for the University of Leicester in England. There, he studied the inherited differences in human DNA in order to map genes and help develop diagnoses for inherited diseases.

Most human DNA is identical in everyone—99.9 percent! But each person has about 100,000 genes made up of about 3 billion nucleotides. So even the tiny 0.1 percent difference from person to person equals 3 million different arrangements. These 3 million unique sequences are scattered throughout the DNA. Scientists had accidently run across these fractions of segments of DNA that were different. Called hypervariable regions, they did not appear to have any function, but Jeffreys hoped to map them.

# THE BREAKTHROUGH

On the morning of September 15, 1984, Jeffreys had prepared specially designed genetic markers of hypervariable DNA to search out regions like themselves. He made them radioactive so they would be visible on X-ray film. As he pulled an X-ray from the developing tank, he exclaimed, "What have we got here!" He had been expecting to see a few random images. Instead there was a series of gray and black bands, much like the bar code put on items in stores.

Each person's "bar code" looks different. These individual sections were the key to making genetic identifications, and Edwin Southern's technique made getting to those regions possible. With Jeffreys's discovery, scientists would be able to readily pinpoint the sections of DNA sequencing that were unique to each individual (with the exception of identical twins).

Jeffreys, his technician Vicky Wilson, and the rest of his team were excited about their find. That morning, they discussed its possible uses for forensic identification, paternity testing, and medical tests relating to transplants and bone marrow grafts. They realized that it could even be used in natural history studies on animals and birds. In the afternoon, they pricked their fingers to make blood smears on tissue and glass in order to test the new technique, which they had named DNA fingerprinting.

This new tool was put to work right away. Jeffreys was asked to help establish a teenager's identity for an immigration case. The teenager was from a family of Ghanaians who had become British subjects. When the teenager tried to return to Britain from a visit to Ghana, suspicious immigration officials kept him from coming into the country.

Conventional blood typing methods were not useful in this case because the teen's father was unknown. To prove that the teen was indeed a member of the family he said he belonged to, Jeffreys took blood from the boy, his mother, and her three other children. He made DNA fingerprints of the mother and the three other siblings. As humans inherit about half their genetic makeup from each parent, DNA fingerprints of family members should have some of the same DNA segments.

As it turned out, the young man's DNA fingerprint matched the mother's and he was proved to be a member of the family. Jeffreys personally told the mother that the case had been dropped against her son. "It was a golden moment to see the look on that poor woman's face when she heard that her two-year nightmare had ended," he said.

This case was important for Jeffreys for a scientific reason as well. Although his method worked well in this instance, he realized that to make an accurate DNA fingerprint, he would need more high-quality DNA than could often be found at crime scenes. He set about refining his process, which is called RFLP (restriction fragment length polymorphism) or "Riflips." His improved process made the patterns easier to read and possible to store in a computer database. And these profiles could also be made with less DNA.

## THE RESULT

DNA profiling was ready and waiting to be tried in forensics work when police investigators called on Jeffreys to help them solve two cases. Two teenagers, Lynda Mann and Dawn Ashworth, had been raped and killed in a village not far from the University of Leicester, where Jeffreys worked. Although Lynda had been killed in 1983 and Dawn was murdered in 1986, the crimes were similar enough that the police believed their murders were committed by the same person. A massive search for the killer turned up a

*Kath Eastwood holds a photograph of her 15-year-old daughter, Lynda Mann, who was murdered while walking to a friend's home one cold November evening in 1983.*

man, George Howard, who confessed to murdering Dawn. Although he had admitted only the second murder, police officers wondered if he had also killed Lynda and suggested that DNA fingerprinting be done.

Jeffreys tested DNA from semen found at both of the crime scenes and compared it to Howard's DNA. The results were unexpected. As the police had suspected, the semen samples belonged to the same man—but not to George Howard, who had confessed! The police undertook a large DNA fingerprinting sweep of all the young men in the area. The police did not really expect the murderer to step forward and be tested, but hoped instead to flush him out. Most of the young men—4,582 of them—from the three small villages complied and donated blood. But there was no match.

The break in the case came when a witness reported overhearing a conversation in a pub about a man named Colin Pitchfork who had paid someone to give blood for the DNA test in his name. When the police went to Pitchfork to retest him, he confessed to the crimes. His DNA sample did match. Old-fashioned detective work, in the form of following up on a tip, was vital to this case, but DNA testing made a difference as well.

This was the first case in which DNA testing proved a person's innocence, as well as another's guilt, but it wasn't the last. "If we hadn't developed the technology, I'm confident [the first suspect] would have been jailed for life," Jeffreys commented. "[DNA profiling has] led to a swathe of longstanding

---

DNA can be found in every nucleated cell in a person's body. A nucleated cell has a nucleus—and most cells have one. The DNA in one cell is exactly the same as in every other cell.

convictions around the world being overturned. Some of these people had been in jail for over a decade before molecular evidence proved their innocence."

In a United States Department of Justice study, "Convicted by Juries, Exonerated by Science," former Attorney General Janet Reno wrote, "With

*Jeffreys's technique showed such potential that England's first commercial DNA-fingerprinting lab, Cellmark Diagnostics, opened in 1987.*

[one] exception . . . the [28] individuals whose stories are told in the report were convicted after jury trials and were sentenced to long prison terms. They successfully challenged their convictions using DNA tests on existing evidence. They had served, on average, seven years in prison."

DNA testing has become more standardized over the years and results have become more accepted in courts. In 1988, another technique was developed that required less DNA. Kari Mullis, Henry Erlich, and others invented the polymerase chain reaction (PCR) amplification method. With PCR, very small amounts of DNA can be copied in order to make enough DNA to be tested.

Jeffreys used PCR in 1990 on skeletal remains believed to be those of Josef Mengele, a notorious Nazi war criminal from Auschwitz known as the "Angel of Death." After World War II, Mengele escaped to South America. He was hunted for decades, but never caught. Many people wanted to know what became of Mengele, but without a positive identification, there would never be resolution. A DNA test comparing the bones to DNA from Mengele's mother and his son showed that it was indeed Mengele's skeleton. Finally, the case was closed.

In 1995, Britain took DNA identification of criminals one step further, initiating the first national criminal DNA database. When people are convicted of serious offenses, their DNA profile is taken and stored. "If they reoffend and leave biological evidence, they can be apprehended," Jeffreys said.

---

DNA can even be extracted from the saliva left on the back of a postage stamp or on a beverage can.

Alec Jeffreys (right) announced to the media the results of the genetic tests he performed on remains believed to be Nazi war criminal Josef Mengele (below). Found in Brazil in 1979, the remains did prove to be the long-sought Mengele. Also on hand to announce the conclusion of this case was German prosecutor Hans Eberhard Klein (left).

*DNA research and testing have dramatically changed how doctors treat patients, how anthropologists study the past, and how scientists view the world, as well as how forensic experts solve crimes.*

"The DNA information of 250,000 people is now stored on that database and it's already proved very successful at linking unsolved crimes, identifying possible perpetrators, and giving police new leads." In the U.S., the FBI initiated a DNA database in 1998. The state of Virginia also makes DNA profiles of all convicted felons. Using computers, law enforcement officials can compare these profiles to

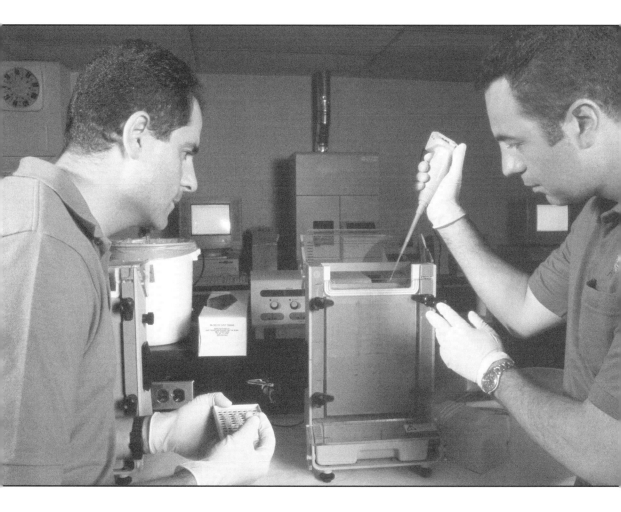

DNA collected at crime scenes. By 2001, many states were beginning to create DNA databases.

Alec Jeffreys, meanwhile, continues his professorship with the University of Leicester. In 1994, he was knighted for his "services to genetics." His current studies focus on DNA mutation—changes that occur when DNA is transmitted from one generation to the next. In connection with that work, he has investigated the genetic effects on the people exposed to radiation during the 1986 nuclear power plant disaster at Chernobyl, Ukraine.

Being able to create a genetic profile of a person from a small amount of evidence is an enormously useful development that some see as the most exciting and important law enforcement tool of the twentieth century. That this breakthrough came about by accident while Jeffreys was researching something else is typical of science. The ability to apply that new knowledge can be as important as having discovered it. We may not know the full impact of Sir Alec Jeffreys's work for many years to come.

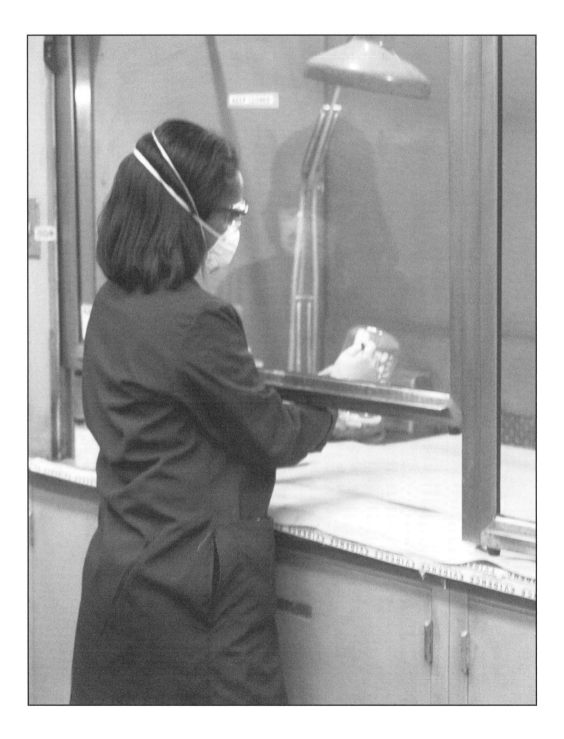

# Forensics in the Future: Trends and Technology

It takes hard work to keep up with criminals. As John H. Wigmore, Dean of Northwestern University's law school, noted in 1910, "in each age, crime takes advantage of conditions, and then society awakes and gradually overtakes crime." There's no doubt that the future of forensics holds serious challenges to be faced, but it also has endless possibilities.

The many methods that forensic scientists find to identify suspects are intriguing as well as ingenious. For example, in the 1990s, the FBI was up against a gang that was robbing banks and detonating bombs in the Spokane, Washington, area. One gang member was filmed during a robbery in 1996. Although he wore a mask that hid his face entirely, determined and resourceful FBI scientists found another way to place the suspect at the scene.

The criminal's denim jeans had been caught on film and the FBI discovered that the wear on his jeans had a visible pattern. Slight imperfections occur in

*Even the tried-and-true method of powdering for fingerprints has grown more sophisticated, as demonstrated by this technician in the FBI's latent print laboratory.*

the assembly of blue jeans. Because people often wear their jeans until the fabric grows thin, these patterns are more obvious on jeans than on other pants. The scientists looked at the jeans of all of the suspects in the case and compared them with the pair that had been filmed. The filmed jeans had a pattern with over two dozen notable features. Jeans worn by one of the suspects matched those features, and he was charged with the crime. At the trial, defense lawyers brought in 34 similar pairs of blue jeans, claiming that it was impossible to distinguish one pair of worn jeans from another. But the FBI expert was able to identify the defendant's jeans from among the samples. The accused man was convicted based on this evidence.

Images—such as photographs or videotape—are a vital part of police work, as the previous example indicates, but they offer their own challenges. The ability of computers to alter images is useful to forensic specialists who want to re-create a suspect's face from a witness's memory, but it presents a difficulty for police officers who want their photographic evidence to be trusted in courts.

Companies such as Epson are working on a solution to the problem of digital photograph authentication. Epson has developed a software program called the Image Authentication System that designates images as "authentic" or "inauthentic." Inauthentic images are ones that have been changed in any way.

Other devices called mass spectroscopes have become very valuable to forensics and hold promise

**digital photography:** a method of photography in which an image is converted into numbers and stored for reproduction

for future forensic tests. These various types of instruments can identify the kinds of particles present in a given substance by separating particles of different masses using magnetic or electric fields or both. Mass spectrometry tests are regularly conducted to detect the presence of drugs or of substances used to intentionally set fires, such as explosives and accelerants.

Oak Ridge National Laboratory chemist Michelle Buchanan has applied the mass spectrometry process to advance fingerprinting technology. A mysterious abduction/murder case in 1994 prompted police officer Art Bohanon to ask if children's fingerprints fade more quickly than adult prints. To answer his question, Michelle Buchanan ran mass spectrometry tests and discovered that children's fingerprints contain more volatile chemicals than adult prints. This information indicated that, yes, children's prints don't last as long. Buchanan then set to work on creating a special child-sensitive fingerprint kit.

Mass spectrometry also has the potential to disclose details about the source of fingerprints, such as levels of nicotine, cholesterol, and other substances that the person had in his or her body when the prints were made.

In their efforts to solve crimes, detectives may sometimes turn to unexpected places for help. Fields that do not seem to have a forensic aspect, such as botany and entomology, can turn out to be instrumental in a case. For instance, entomology—the study of insects—can yield critical information to crime solving, particularly regarding time of death of decomposing bodies.

In a murder case in suburban Washington, D.C., for example, the police had sizable evidence pointing to a particular suspect, but they needed to know when the victim died. The body had been lying in the woods for possibly as long as 18 days. Entomologists studied the blowflies present on the body and calculated, based on the weather conditions and the insects' stage of development, that the body had been there for 15 days. This conclusion was later confirmed by the confession of the arrested suspect.

Botany, the study of plants, was helpful in a 1991 murder case in Minnesota. A suspect, who was a coworker of the murdered woman, had been found near her home, his car stuck in a ditch. He claimed the woman was already dead when he stopped by to repay a debt. Police found the murder weapon in the woods behind her house. They also found grass and shrubbery in the suspect's shoes and pant cuffs. They asked University of Minnesota botanist Anita Cholewa to evaluate this plant evidence. Her analysis showed that the plant material matched that growing in the victim's backyard, where the murderer had to have walked to dispose of the weapon. The suspect was convicted and sentenced to life in prison. Cholewa has helped the police in a dozen different cases since. "I'm trained to recognize patterns and which patterns go together," she said of her detection work. "They lead you to identify a plant, even if it is in tiny pieces."

One of the most notable challenges facing forensic scientists today is how to handle computer crime. Law enforcement organizations must find a way to deal with problems that range from decoding encrypted computer files that contain key evidence about terrorist activities to tracking down child

*Anita Cholewa searches through the University of Minnesota's collection of more than 850,000 dried and pressed plants.*

pornographers using the Internet to protecting intellectual property from sophisticated computer hackers.

Computers may be a source of challenge for crime solvers, but the use of computers in forensic work will continue to be a boon to law enforcement. Increased development of computer databases that contain evidence records will make it easier for law enforcement officers and forensic specialists to find information they need. Some databases, however, such as DNA profiles, raise ethical questions about maintaining citizen privacy.

Notably, one of the major ways forensics is likely to change in the future is not due to new technology. Although in the past, individual judges have been able to decide what makes acceptable evidence and who is enough of an expert to offer it, today many in the legal profession are seeking standardization of forensics. Advocates of standardization argue that if forensic evidence is to be consistently reliable, forensic specialists need to be certified and to work in accredited laboratories using prescribed methods. Once these efforts are accomplished, there's no telling what forensics can achieve.

# GLOSSARY

**anthropology:** a scientific study of the origin, behavior, and the physical, social, and cultural development of human beings

**anthropometry:** the study of human body measurement used by anthropologists to compare and classify human beings; from the Greek words *anthropos* (human being) and *metron* (measure)

**antidote:** a substance that acts against the effects of a poison

**arsenic:** a silvery semimetallic element found in sulfide or metallic ores, such as copper and lead. Poisonous to humans, arsenic was a popular method of murder until the twentieth century.

**autopsy:** post-mortem (after death) examination of a body, usually by a doctor who specializes in this branch of science, known as a medical examiner

**ballistics:** the study of thrown or propelled objects in flight. The term can apply to the travel paths of spacecraft or large missiles, but in forensics the term refers to bullets and the guns that fire them.

**botany:** the study of plants

**cadaver:** a dead body, especially one intended for dissection

**caliber:** the diameter of the inside of the barrel of a firearm, usually measured in hundredths or thousandths of an inch and written as a decimal fraction, such as .45 caliber

**caustics:** substances capable of burning, corroding, or dissolving by chemical action

**cell:** the smallest unit of living things. The cell is made up of a substance called protoplasm and surrounded by a thin membrane. Most cells have a central part called a nucleus surrounded by a clear fluid called cytoplasm. In many-celled animals and plants, such as humans and trees, different types of cells have specific functions.

**chromosome:** the tiny, thread-like parts in the nucleus of a cell that carry the genes of heredity

**comparison microscope:** a microscope with two lenses that can display their contents side by side at equal magnification for accurate comparison

**dactylography:** the study of fingerprints as a method of identification

**decompose:** to break down into components; to decay or cause to rot

**digital photography:** a method of photography in which an image is converted into numbers and stored for reproduction

**DNA (deoxyribonucleic acid):** a nucleic acid that carries the genetic information in the cell; it consists of two long chains of nucleotides twisted into a double helix and joined by hydrogen bonds; the sequence of bases in nucleotides determines individual hereditary characteristics. *See also* **chromosome, gene, nucleotide, nucleus**

**electromagnetism:** forces of attraction and repulsion produced by an electric current

**entomology:** the study of insects

**enzyme:** a complex substance found in living things that controls a chemical reaction without being changed itself. An average cell in the human body contains about 3,000 different enzymes.

**evidence:** anything that could help decide the guilt or innocence of a person suspected of a crime

**fingerprints:** impressions of the ridges on a person's fingertips, formed from perspiration and oils secreted from the small pores on those ridges. *See also* **latent fingerprints, plastic fingerprints, rolled fingerprints, visible (or patent) fingerprints**

**forensics:** science that has been applied to questions of civil and criminal law; from the Latin *for ensis*, meaning "public forum"

**gene:** a tiny part of a chromosome in the nucleus of a cell that is the basic unit of inheritance. A gene determines a particular characteristic in the organism.

**genetics:** the study of heredity

**gunshot residue:** the powder (necessary to propel a bullet from a gun) that does not completely burn when a gun is fired. This leftover powder can remain on the hand of the person who fired the weapon and/or on the target.

**gunsmith:** a person who makes or repairs firearms

**hydrochloric acid:** a clear, highly acidic solution used in chemistry

**hydrogen sulfide:** a colorless, flammable, poisonous gas used in chemistry to detect or measure another substance

**land:** the raised portion of a grooved surface

**latent fingerprints:** fingerprints invisible to the human eye. Latent prints can be found on surfaces such as glass, metal, or wood. A forensics expert can make these prints visible with various powders and other methods.

**mug shot:** a photo of a person charged with a crime

**nucleotide:** a compound consisting of a base, a sugar, and a phosphate group; DNA is made up of nucleotides

**nucleus:** a spherical structure within the cell that controls the cell and its functions; the nucleus contains genetic information for the growth, maintenance, and reproduction of the organism

**perjury:** deliberately giving false testimony under oath, especially in a court proceeding; perjury is a crime

**pistol:** a firearm designed to be held and fired with one hand

**plastic fingerprints:** impressions of fingerprints left in a soft substance such as paint, wax, or chocolate

**revolver:** a pistol having a revolving cylinder with several cartridge chambers that may be fired in succession

**rolled fingerprints:** prints taken from an individual by rolling the finger on an ink pad and then pressing it onto a white card

**Spanish fly:** a green beetle that can be dried and crushed to create a toxic preparation used as an irritant

**spectrometer:** an instrument that measures spectrums, such as the wavelengths of energy or the atomic and subatomic particles of a substance

**sulfuric acid:** a highly corrosive, thick, oily liquid used to manufacture a variety of chemicals and products such as paints and explosives

**topography:** the surface features of a place or region

**toxicology:** the study of poisons—their effects, ways to detect them, and the treatments for poisoning

**visible (or patent) fingerprints:** fingerprints easily seen by the human eye. Someone with dirt, blood, or grease on his or her fingers would leave visible prints.

**X-ray fluorescence spectrometer:** a spectrometer that uses X-rays and fluorescence (the emission of electromagnetic radiation) to separate the chemical parts of a substance so these elements can be identified and measured

**zinc:** a shiny, blue-white metallic element that can be shaped when heated

# BIBLIOGRAPHY

Almirall, Jose R., and Kenneth G. Furton. "The Evolution, Practice and Future of the Use of Science in the Administration of Justice—The Importance of Standards in Forensic Science." *Standardization News*, April 1995.

Campbell, Duncan. "Dandruff Could Collar Criminals." *The Age*, September 17, 1998.

Carter, David L., and Andra J. Katz. "Computer Crime: An Emerging Challenge for Law Enforcement." http://www.fbi.gov/leb/dec961.txt, cited December 1996.

Chadwick, David. "Computer Identification System (CIDS): History, Synopsis and Future Directions." Paper presented at Asia Pacific Police Technology Conference, 1993.

Cohen, Philip. "In Their Jeans." *New Scientist*, February 21, 1998.

Committee on DNA Technology in Forensic Science, National Research Council. *DNA Technology in Forensic Science*. Washington, D.C.: National Academy Press, 1992.

Deutsch, Yvonne, ed. *Science Against Crime*. New York: Exeter Books, 1982.

Dougherty, Paul M. "In Memory of Calvin Hooker Goddard, M.D., Col. U.S. Army." *AFTE Journal*, October 1991.

Eckert, William G., ed. *Introduction to Forensic Sciences*. Boca Raton, Fla.: CRC Press, 1997.

Evans, Colin. *The Casebook of Forensic Detection: How Science Solved 100 of the World's Most Baffling Crimes*. New York: John Wiley & Sons, 1996.

Franklin-Barbajosa, Cassandra. "DNA Profiling: The New Science of Identity." *National Geographic*, May 1992.

Fridell, Ron. *Solving Crimes: Pioneers of Forensic Science*. New York: Franklin Watts, 2000.

*Frye v. United States*, 293 F2d 1073 (D.C. Cir. 1923).

Graysmith, Robert. *Unabomber: A Desire to Kill.* Washington, D.C.: Regnery Publishing, 1997.

Joyce, Christopher, and Eric Stover. *Witnesses From The Grave.* Boston: Little, Brown, 1991.

Kaye, Brian H. *Science and the Detective.* New York: John Wiley & Sons, 1995.

Kind, Stuart, and Michael Overman. *Science Against Crime.* Garden City, N.Y.: Doubleday, 1972.

Kurland, Michael. *How To Solve a Murder: The Forensic Handbook.* New York: Macmillan, 1995.

Lagerkvist, Ulf. *DNA Pioneers and Their Legacy.* New Haven, Conn.: Yale University Press, 1998.

Lee, Henry C., and R. D. Gaensslen, eds. *Advances in Fingerprint Technology.* Boca Raton, Fla.: CRC Press, 1994.

Levy, Harlan. *And The Blood Cried Out.* New York: BasicBooks, 1996.

Lord, Philip. "Case Histories of the Use of Insects in Investigations." Federal Bureau of Investigations, Washington, D.C.

Machrone, Bill. "Digital Image Authentication Hits the Consumer Market." *PCWeek Online*, April 26, 1999.

Manheim, Mary H. *The Bone Lady.* Baton Rouge: Louisiana State University Press, 1999.

Maples, William R., and Michael Browning. *Dead Men Do Tell Tales.* New York: Doubleday, 1994.

Newton, Michael. *The Encyclopedia of Serial Killers.* New York: Facts on File, 2000.

Osborn, Albert S. *Questioned Documents.* Albany, N.Y.: Boyd Printing, 1929.

Pejsa, Jane. *The Molineux Affair.* Minneapolis: Kenwood, 1983.

Penry, Jacques. *Looking at Faces and Remembering Them: A Guide to Facial Identification.* London: Elek Books, 1971.

———. "Photo-Fit." *The Criminologist,* 1974.

Rhine, Stanley. *Bone Voyage.* Albuquerque: University of New Mexico Press, 1998.

Saferstein, Richard, ed. *Forensic Science Handbook.* Englewood Cliffs, N.J.: Prentice-Hall, 1982.

Tesar, Jenny. *Scientific Crime Investigation.* New York: Franklin Watts, 1991.

Thorwald, Jurgen. *The Century of the Detective.* New York: Harcourt, 1965.

Ullyett, Kenneth. *Criminology.* London: Franklin Watts, 1972.

Wilton, George Wilton. *Fingerprints: History, Law, and Romance.* Ann Arbor, Mich.: Gryphon Books, 1971.

Zonderman, Jon. *Beyond the Crime Lab: The New Science of Investigation.* New York: John Wiley & Sons, 1990.

## ABOUT THE AUTHOR

**Tabatha Yeatts**, born in Virginia in 1970, graduated from Mary Washington College, Fredericksburg, Virginia, with a bachelor's degree in English and from the University of Iowa with a master's degree in communications studies. Yeatts has written *The Holocaust Survivors*, as well as articles and short stories for publications ranging from *Cricket* to *Murderous Intent Magazine*. She belongs to the Short Mystery Fiction Society and Sisters in Crime. This is her first book for The Oliver Press. She lives with her family in Maryland.

## PHOTO ACKNOWLEDGEMENTS